The Journals of Captain John Smith

THE JOURNALS OF CAPTAIN JOHN SMITH

A JAMESTOWN BIOGRAPHY

EDITED BY JOHN M. THOMPSON

NATIONAL GEOGRAPHIC
ADVENTURE CLASSICS

WASHINGTON, D.C.

Excerpts from *The Complete Works of Captain John Smith (1580-1631)*, edited by Philip L. Barbour (Chapel Hill: University of North Carolina Press for the Omohundro Institute of Early American History and Culture), copyright © 1986 by the University of North Carolina Press. Reprinted by permission of the publisher. *www.uncpress.unc.edu*

ISBN-10 1-4262-0055-2
ISBN-13 978-1-4262-0055-7

Printed in U.S.A.

Library of Congress Cataloging-in-Publication Data

Smith, John, 1580-1631.
    [Journals. Selections]
    The journals of Captain John Smith : a Jamestown biography / edited by John M. Thompson.
        p. cm. – (Adventure classics)
    Includes index.
    ISBN 978-1-4262-0055-7 (pbk. : alk. paper)
    1. Smith, John, 1580-1631–Diaries. 2. Colonists–Virginia–Diaries. 3. Explorers–America–Diaries. 4. Explorers–Great Britain–Diaries. 5. Jamestown (Va.)–History–17th century. 6. Jamestown (Va.)–Biography. 7. Virginia–History–Colonial period, ca. 1600-1775. 8. Chesapeake Bay Region (Md. and Va.)–Discovery and exploration. I. Thompson, John M. (John Milliken), 1959- II. Title.
    F229.S7A3 2007
    973.2'1092–dc22
    [B]
                        2006036577

One of the world's largest nonprofit scientific and educational organizations, the National Geographic Society was founded in 1888 "for the increase and diffusion of geographic knowledge." Fulfilling this mission, the Society educates and inspires millions every day through its magazines, books, television programs, videos, maps and atlases, research grants, the National Geographic Bee, teacher workshops, and innovative classroom materials. The Society is supported through membership dues, charitable gifts, and income from the sale of its educational products. This support is vital to National Geographic's mission to increase global understanding and promote conservation of our planet through exploration, research, and education.

For more information, please call 1-800-NGS LINE (647-5463) or write to the following address:

NATIONAL GEOGRAPHIC SOCIETY
1145 17th Street N.W.
Washington, DC 20036-4688 U.S.A.

Visit the Society's Web site at www.nationalgeographic.com/books

CONTENTS

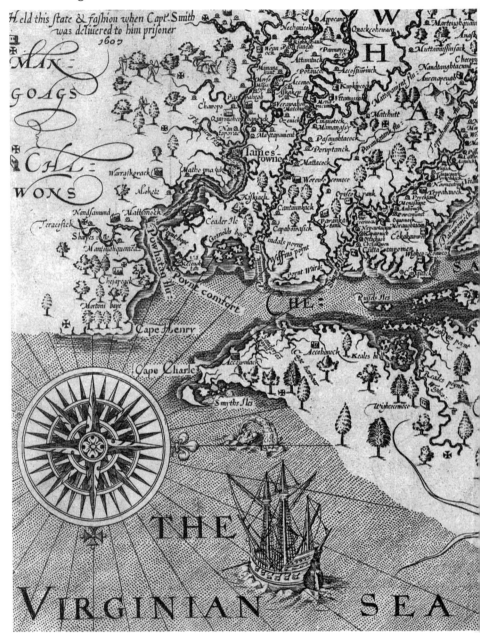

CHESAPEAKE BAY AND SURROUNDS IN JOHN SMITH'S 1612 MAP OF
VIRGINIA (NORTH ON RIGHT), BASED ON SKETCHES BY SMITH

THE PORTRAICTVER OF CAPTAYNE IOHN SMITH · ADMIRALL OF NEW ENGLAND.

These are the Lines that shew thy Face; but those
That shew thy Grace and Glory, brighter bee:
Thy Faire Discoueries and FOWLE-Overthrowes
Of Salvages, much Civilliz'd by thee
Best shew thy Spirit; and to it GLORY Wyn
So, thou art Brasse without, but Golde within.

Published by W. Richardson Castle Street Leicester Fields.

CAPTAIN JOHN SMITH (FROM HIS MAP
OF NEW ENGLAND, 1616)

INTRODUCTION

BY JOHN M. THOMPSON

IN LATE DECEMBER 1606 the *Susan Constant* and two smaller ships eased from the Thames River and out toward the Atlantic. The 144 passengers and crew were embarked upon a daring mission. If they succeeded, they would be rich and famous for life; if they failed, they would die. Their goal was to set up an outpost in a place called Virginia, which was about as well known as any named feature on the moon. Spain had nominally claimed it—along with thousands of miles of Atlantic coastline—based on cursory explorations. Going on hunches, hearsay, and opinions on good latitudes, a group of investors called the Virginia Company of London reckoned that Virginia would be the perfect location to find precious metals—namely, gold and silver. While there, the colonists could also probably find a shortcut to the Pacific and thus bring more profits through trade with the Orient. The venture was, in short, no grand vision of America from sea to shining sea but a get-rich-quick scheme. But even if no riches materialized, the outmaneuvering of Spain for global dominance was justification enough.

Nineteen years earlier, a nascent English colony along the coast of present-day North Carolina had simply vanished, the "Lost Colony" likely destroyed or absorbed by local Indian tribes. Now the British, the only European power without a foothold in the New World, were going to try again. Most of the people on the 1606 voyage had no intention of putting down roots in Virginia. Like the California gold-seekers nearly 250 years later, they planned to stay a year or two and then take their booty home. They could not know that most of them would perish and that only one would become famous, though not wealthy.

His name was as common as his birth. Twenty-six-year-old John Smith was born a yeoman farmer's son in eastern England. He was short, stocky, dark-haired, confident, and endowed with a lust for adventure. He tried to run away from home at age 13; three years later he was gone. For the next several years he journeyed restlessly over Europe and Asia, serving as a soldier of fortune for the Dutch against the Spanish, then with the Austrians against the Turks. Honing his native intelligence in the school of experience, he learned how to fight on land and at sea, how to size up and bluff an enemy, and when to put his bravery and strength to the test—all skills he would need in the hostile American wilderness. The Austrians, at one point in his young career, gave him command of 250 horsemen, with whom he captured a walled city. At another time he dueled three Turks in as many days, and, with pistol, battle-ax, and sword, killed them all. Finally his luck ran out and he was captured and sold into slavery in Constantinople. Seizing a chance, he killed his master, stole the latter's horse, and escaped to Russia. Various escapades later, he made his way back to England.

Casting about for his next adventure, Smith was the right person in the right place in 1606. Members of the Virginia Company had heard about Smith and his exploits. Never one to shy from self-publicity, the swaggering full-bearded young gamecock had made himself known. In addition to a new play titled *Macbeth*, Smith might well have seen *Eastward Hoe* at Blackfriars theater and heard that Virginia was "as pleasant a country as ever the sun shined on." And he probably knew poet Michael Drayton's incitement, "To get the pearl and gold / And ours to hold / VIRGINIA / Earth's only paradise."

So it was that Smith boarded the 116-foot flagship bound for Virginia. Well before the four-month trip was over, he had made friends—and enemies. The long voyage in crowded conditions, with scant rations that turned stale and rancid, inevitably led to illness and bickering and the kind of splintering into factions that would make a modern reality show pale in comparison. Many of the high-born gentlemen on board thought Smith rude and arrogant—likely they felt somewhat outmatched by his tales of bravado. He had so alienated himself from the gentry that by the time the expedition reached its destination, he was under arrest and sentenced to death. Imagine their surprise and dismay when on arrival in Virginia, per company instructions, a sealed box containing the names of the colony's leaders was opened. Not every name was appreciated.

The fleet entered the mouth of the Chesapeake Bay and headed up the closest large river, which they named the James after their king. After scouting around, the colonists chose a spot on which to begin a settlement. The first job, on May 13, 1607, was to open the sealed box. Among the names on the list was that of one-armed Capt. Christopher Newport, commander of the Atlantic crossing and veteran of raids on the Spanish West Indies. Also listed were the captains of the escort ships, Bartholomew Gosnold and John Ratcliffe, the latter a schemer particularly loathed by Smith. There was also a lawyer, a soldier, and a vague figure later suspected of being an informant to the Spanish. The seventh name, and youngest of the leaders, was John Smith. The other leaders voted immediately to exclude him from the Council.

Then the real work began. Before any hunting for gold could start, the settlers had to dig in—clear trees, build a fortified post, plant crops, and try to keep from dying of exhaustion and sickness. In essence they were a military expedition working for a trading company; after seven years (if they survived and stayed) they could own land and receive other benefits. Though briefly hassled by local Indians, the settlers found the first few months, if not paradisal, at least promising. The settlement of Jamestown was situated on a little peninsula about 60 miles up from Cape Henry. The land appeared fertile and full of game; the waters held giant crabs, mussels, oysters, and an abundance of fish; the pine forests promised pitch and tar, the hardwoods timber and masts; the climate was healthy. Spring was a good time to have arrived in tidewater Virginia.

The settlers knuckled down to work—planting wheat and, above all, digging. As ludicrous as it sounds today, these pioneers were convinced by Indian rumors that plenty of gold lay around for the taking. They began loading the ships with dirt, which they called "ore." In the meantime, John Smith argued his way out of the death sentence and back onto the Council. The colony needed strong backs and hearty constitutions, and if anybody possessed these, it was Smith. Yet he soon had doubts about the focus of the labor. He was among the few (he maintained in retrospect) who thought the labor would be better spent settling in and discovering what the area's true natural resources were.

But they kept digging, fueled by tales of the conquistadors, who had found mineral riches in South America. Greed made the colonists believe, and belief kept them working. It was not long, though, before the real disadvantage of Jamestown's location became apparent. The lack of gold was not the problem. The settlement was built beside a swamp that contained brackish water; the tainted drinking water weakened the overworked settlers, many of whom then became seriously ill. Even Smith, strong as he was, became sick for a while. By early July only a few settlers were well; a month later people began dying. As the food supply dwindled and the weather became brutally hot, the death toll rose. By September half of the entire colony was dead.

All along, the Indians had been a thorny problem, and as the colony wavered and finally held out against disease and starvation, they became the main threat to Jamestown's survival. Newport and other leaders were determined that a friendly, ingratiating attitude would work much better than the Spanish model of total domination. But a cultural clash was inevitable. The language barrier made for constant misunderstandings, and religious differences were tremendous. While the English did not feel the Indians were lower life-forms, they did perceive them as untutored primitives or "savages" on the order of wild children who were not yet civilized. Further complicating the picture, local tribes began using the whites as leverage against each other—the friendship showed toward one tribe was often taken as a hostile move by another.

John Smith came to Virginia the most prepared of the settlers; he had done his homework, studying the reports from Raleigh's failed colony and learning some Algonquian phrases.

And so Smith's Virginia story begins in the spring of 1607 and continues until the fall of 1609. During those two and a half years, he would match wits and arms with the powerful ruler Powhatan, become embroiled with Powhatan's daughter Pocahontas, suppress mutinies, and keep the young colony from being wiped off the map. His story is one of operatic complexity, filled with riveting accounts of battle, intrigue, revenge, betrayal, romance, and death. It is the story of a new world.

A NOTE ON THE TEXT

A GOODLY PART OF THE REASON John Smith's name is writ large across early Virginia is that he himself did the writing. He emerges as the hero, because he was the one who took the time and bother to write the history.

Now comes the rub. Smith published several books in his lifetime, but the content is not all his own. As was common during his time, Smith borrowed the writings—published and unpublished—of other colonists and historians and reworked them into his own books. There are no extant "journals" in Smith's hand; instead there are Smith's books in which he often, but not always, credits other writers. In many cases he may not have known who wrote what. In any event, it is impossible most of the time to know exactly what came from Smith's pen and what he borrowed. Suffice it to say that, as a compiler, he at least edited everything that he himself did not write. We are left, then, with books under John Smith's name, written in a blunt but vigorous style, with a natural storyteller's gift for the telling detail. The grain ceremony during his captivity, for instance, is so rich that you can smell and hear the life of primitive tidewater Virginia; these scenes, by the way, have to be from Smith's hand since he was the only Englishman there. Later on, the scene with Pocahontas and her friends is a small gem of comic erotica.

Smith's first publication took the form of a letter of about 40 pages, written to the Virginia Company. It was published without his knowledge or consent in London in 1608 under the title *A True Relation of Such Occurrences and Accidents of Note as Hath Happened in Virginia*. References to bickering and hardships were edited out so that investors would not be scared off.

Three years after his return from Virginia, Smith published *A Map of Virginia, with a Description of the Country, the Commodities,*

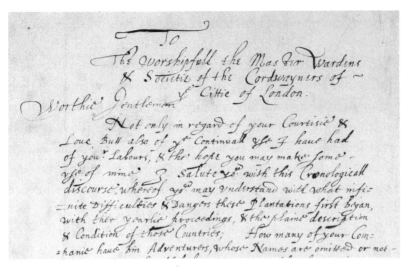

FRAGMENT OF A RARE SURVIVING INSCRIPTION WRITTEN BY SMITH
IN A COPY OF HIS *GENERAL HISTORY,* 1624

People, Government and Religion (1612) and a companion volume
entitled *The Proceedings of the English Colony in Virginia since Their
First Beginning from England in the Year of Our Lord 1606* (1612).
The latter book offers a more complete account of early Jamestown than *A True Relation,* and definitely uses other sources since
its scope extends beyond Smith's time in Virginia. No longer in
the employ of the Company, Smith had begun to criticize colony
management freely. Two books about Smith's New England ventures followed in 1616 and 1620, both with uncharacteristically
short titles.

Smith next turned out his longest title yet, his magnum opus,
*The General History of Virginia, New England, and the Summer Isles:
with the Names of the Adventurers, Planters, and Governors from Their
First Beginning An: 1584 to This Present 1624* (1624). A work in six vol-
umes, the *General History* covers the entire British American enterprise, beginning with Sir Walter Raleigh's colonization efforts and
continuing up to the time of publication. Interspersed with detailed

illustrations, maps, and laudatory poems by friends, the book was well received, and it bolstered the spirits of an author whose ego needed much stroking. The important thing for his English readers, though, was that the book gave them a sweeping account of their nation's grappling with the conquest of a continent. Book 3, from which most of The Journals of Captain John Smith is taken, is an almost line-for-line reprint of The Proceedings. The rambling Book 4 carries the Jamestown story beyond the Smith era. Smith continued to write until his death, publishing an autobiography, two works on seafaring, and another book on colonization.

Text for the book you hold is from the monumental three-volume The Complete Works of Captain John Smith (1580-1631), edited by Philip L. Barbour (University of North Carolina Press, 1986). Barbour's painstaking scholarship takes the all but unreadable original text and renders it into comprehensible English. Gone is the florid typeface; "vv" is changed to "w"; "j" and "v" are altered to represent consonants only; the old form of "s" that looked like an "f" no longer does; italicized words are set in roman. These and numerous other changes make clear what Smith intended.

To accommodate the modern lay reader, the present volume goes a step or two further. Barbour retains Smith's wildly inconsistent spellings and classical punctuation. The word "arrow" might be spelled "Arrow," "arrowe," "Arrowe," or "arrow" all within a single paragraph. All spellings here have been standardized. In Smith's day a subject could be separated from a verb by a comma or semicolon because a breath was in order, and a subject might apply to a long series of dependent clauses strung together with semicolons. Parenthetical material several lines long can cause one to forget the subject. Pronoun referents are often unclear. The present volume uses modern punctuation to ease the reader along, breaking long sentences and paragraphs into shorter ones and clarifying ambiguity where possible.

There are a few cuts within selections, but no additions or rewordings. Occasionally a word or phrase needs a gloss; these are bracketed in italics—"to hull" [*furl sails and drift*]. My summaries and commentaries between sections of text are also set in italics. The few italicized words within the body of the text are Indian words, ship names, or classical poems that Smith borrowed from a book entitled *Atheomastix* (published by Martin Fotherby in 1622). There is one couplet by Smith himself. Dates, by the way, are Old Style— ten days behind the modern calendar.

The resulting text is not a translation, simply a modernization. Smith's original voice still comes through loud and clear, with all its boasting, griping, and high spirits. There is plenty of period flavor without the quaint spellings. If a word is archaic but perfectly clear, I let it stand: hath, keepeth, alarum. Likewise, it was impossible to resist "chickings" for "chickens," and so on. Smith's looping sentences, fragments, and misplaced modifiers take a little getting used to, as does the rhetoric of Jacobean English. But those at all familiar with Shakespeare or the King James Bible will quickly adjust. Unlike his contemporary Shakespeare (1564-1616), Smith was an adventurer first, a writer second, so one has to excuse his grammatical weaknesses. The puns ("extreme extremity") were standard for the period. As for King James I, he ruled from 1603 to 1625; his authorized version of the Bible was published in 1611.

If in a few places you cannot understand exactly what Smith means, you're not alone—neither can the scholars. Most sentences are as plain as day: "Yet were the hearts of the English ever stupid." Scholar Edward Wright Haile suggests reading quickly—Smith's work was, after all, considered light reading in his day.

Mention should be made of the use of first and third person. Smith will often refer to himself as "Smith" or "the captain." It can be confusing or seem boastful. Remember that much of the material was written by Smith's fellow colonists (including all of the post-Smith Jamestown material). There was not a tradition of autobiography or memoir then, so he let the third person stand. Also, presenting his work under multiple authors might have been a way to screen himself from official ire.

The dialogue that Smith reports is not exactly as he remembered it verbatim. It is, as Barbour says, "polished, elaborated, tricked out, for readers used to the volcanic vigor of Shakespeare, Ben Jonson," and others. Yet it has an immediacy and vibrancy that makes it feel real; certainly he captured the spirit of the conversation.

The hundreds of pages Smith wrote, many of them promoting colonization, earned him very little. He was stung by the ingratitude. But he continued writing, with a flair that made him one of England's most popular historians of the time. Over and over he stressed his firm belief that England had a brilliant future in America if she could send industrious settlers, apply wise government, and study the examples of successful colonies set up by the likes of Spain, Portugal, and France. Smith's maps and descriptions were so detailed and accurate they were copied or adapted into every major geological publication on Virginia in the 17th century and used as late as 1873 in negotiations on the boundary between Virginia and Maryland.

Though not an American by birth, John Smith gave us the first great piece of American travel writing. Not until William Bartram's *Travels* in 1791 would a true American-born travel literature emerge. By then the Virginia John Smith knew was long gone, the Indians scattered beyond the mountains, the British flags replaced by ones with stars and stripes.

Most of the excerpts included here are from Books 3 and 4 of *The General History* (Barbour, Vol. II, pp. 133-327). The details of Cassen's execution are from *A Map of Virginia* (Barbour, Vol. I, p. 175).

The speculation about Smith marrying Pocahontas is from *The Proceedings* (Barbour, Vol. II, pp. 274-75). Smith's justifications for conquering countries (found in chapter 8) are from *Advertisements* (Barbour, Vol. III, pp. 276-77).

In addition to Barbour's *Complete Works* I have relied on several other excellent books, including Barbour's *The Three Worlds of Captain John Smith*, Alden Vaughn's *American Genesis*, James Horn's *A Land as God Made It*, J. A. Leo Lemay's *The American Dream of Captain John Smith*, Karen Ordahl Kupperman's *Captain John Smith: A Select Edition of His Writings*, David A. Price's *Love and Hate in Jamestown*, Edward Arber's *Travels and Works of Captain John Smith*, John Page Williams's *Chesapeake: Exploring the Water Trail of Captain John Smith*, and Helen C. Rountree's *John Smith's Chesapeake Voyages, 1607-1609*. Edward Wright Haile's *Jamestown Narratives: Eyewitness Accounts of the Virginia Colony, the First Decade: 1607-1617* is a hefty work of especially fine scholarship, presenting modernized versions of many accounts written by early colonists.

Web sites with useful information on modern Jamestown and the Powhatans include: Virginia Wind, www.virginiawind.com; the National Park Service, www.nps.gov/jamc; the Chesapeake Bay Program, www.chesapeakebay.net.info/jsmith.cfm; the Captain John Smith Four Hundred Project, www.johnsmith400.org; and the Chesapeake Bay Foundation, www.cbf.org.

PRINCIPAL FIGURES

CAPT. GABRIEL ARCHER (circa 1575-1609/10), original Jamestown colonist; educated at Cambridge and Gray's Inn; returned to England in 1608; arrived back in Virginia in August 1609 to lead an anti-Smith faction; died during the "starving time" in the winter of 1609-10.

SIR THOMAS DALE (d. 1619), deputy governor and marshal of Virginia 1611-16; known for his tough code of martial laws; died in Java.

SIR THOMAS GATES (circa 1559-1621), governor of Virginia; sailed with Drake when Raleigh's Roanoke colony was rescued; shipwrecked on Bermuda in July 1609; arrived in Virginia in May 1610; returned to England in July, then back to Virginia in 1611, where he stayed for three years; died in the Netherlands.

CAPTAIN BARTHOLOMEW GOSNOLD (circa 1572-1607), explorer and onetime privateer; probably recruited Smith as a colonist; as second under Newport, he commanded the *Godspeed*; an original councillor, he died the first summer in Virginia.

RALPH HAMOR (circa 1589-1626), after shipwrecking on Bermuda, became a councillor in 1611; survived the 1622 massacre.

CAPTAIN GEORGE KENDALL (1570-1607), an original Jamestown councillor; though the details are sketchy, was executed for mutiny.

CAPT. JOHN MARTIN (circa 1567-1632?), an original Jamestown councillor; a contentious figure about whom little is recorded beyond his quarrels, according to Barbour.

NAMONTACK (no known birth or death dates), Powhatan's trusty servant; both helped and gathered intelligence on the English in 1608; was exchanged for Thomas Savage to learn about the English; traveled to England with Newport.

CAPTAIN CHRISTOPHER NEWPORT (1560-1617), mariner; commanded privateers in the West Indies; commanded the original Jamestown expedition in 1607; employed by the East India Company in 1612; died in Java.

OPECHANCANOUGH (d. 1644), younger half-brother of Powhatan; werowance of Pamunkey; briefly succeeded Powhatan and engineered the massacre of 1622; at 90 years or older, led a larger massacre in 1644 and was captured; killed in prison by a soldier.

Pocahontas (circa 1595-1617), favorite daughter of Powhatan; famously saved Smith's life twice; brought peace between the English and Indians by marrying Rolfe; died in England of pulmonary congestion from London's polluted air.

Powhatan (circa 1540-1618), overlord of tidewater Virginia; named for his chief fortified village near the James River falls; headquartered in Werowocomoco on the Pamunkey (York) River; controlled some 25 villages by conquest.

Captain John Ratcliffe (1570s-1609), alias John Sicklemore (perhaps his real name); master of the pinnace *Discovery* on the original voyage; colony councillor; aligned with Smith at first, then opposed; killed by Indians.

John Rolfe (1585-1622), pioneer tobacco planter; shipwrecked in Bermuda and arrived in Jamestown in June 1610; married Pocahontas around April 5, 1614; returned to England in 1616; his son, Thomas, stayed behind when he came back to Virginia in 1617; served on the Council in 1619; died in 1622, probably before the massacre.

Matthew Scrivener (1580-1609), first new council member in 1608; loyal friend and assistant to Smith, though later disagreed with some decisions; drowned on a canoe trip.

Captain John Smith (1580-1631), key founder of Virginia; original councillor; Jamestown president 1608-09; returned to England in 1609; in 1614 made a final voyage, exploring the "north Virginia" coast, which he named New England; spent the rest of his life tirelessly writing, promoting colonization; died unmarried on June 21, 1631.

Thomas West, Baron De La Warr (1577-1618), member of the Virginia Company in 1609; made governor and captain-general of Virginia for life in 1610; sick, he returned to England in 1611; died sailing back to Virginia in 1618.

Edward Maria Wingfield (circa 1560-1613), member of the Virginia Company; first president of the Council in Jamestown; proved ineffective and unpopular as a colonist and administrator; sailed back to England in 1608.

CHAPTER ONE

Into the Land of Pocahontas

May 13, 1606, to January 1, 1608

A SKIRMISH UPON THE SETTLERS' ARRIVAL *was followed by weeks of relative calm. Then, when Newport, Smith, and 22 others were out exploring the James, a party of 200 warriors attacked the settlement, killed a boy, and wounded several others. The original idea that a strong fort would create distrust was thereafter tossed aside. By mid-June Jamestown had a triangular wooden fort, and anyone who ventured far beyond risked getting picked off by arrows. When Newport took off for England that first summer, Smith, a quick student of the Algonquian language, was left in charge of Indian negotiations. In the next conflict he would play a pivotal role that would gain him a place in American legend.*

Smith was beginning to piece together that his countrymen had landed in a place controlled by a confederation of more than 30 Powhatan tribes. Though there was some infighting between tribes, chief Powhatan was widely respected and feared among the 15,000 Indians in the Chesapeake area. When Newport left with two ships in the summer of 1607, the Indians backed down a bit and tolerated the existence of the interlopers, even going so far as to bring them food. If they had opted for an all-out attack on Jamestown at that point, the weakened settlement probably would have collapsed. Instead they left the colonists to their own internal bickering. With Newport out of the picture, the leadership fell apart. The council elected the schemer Ratcliffe president, but Smith claimed that in fact he himself was really in charge of daily operations.

Smith took six men down to the mouth of the James to trade hatchets and copper for food. The Indians there at first scoffed at these miserable, hungry white men. Smith's answer was to fire off a few rounds to show them he could take whatever he wanted. The Indians promptly began loading Smith's boat with venison, turkeys, and bread, then danced in a show of friendship. Right away Smith established a pattern of fair but firm dealings that he was to maintain with the Indians for his whole stint in America. He was always clear that he was there on business, not to make friends.

After a few more provision-gathering trips, Smith decided to go exploring up the Chickahominy River, which flowed into the James six miles up from the settlement. Ratcliffe was more than glad to be rid of his cocky rival for a while. Smith's crew took a barge as far upriver as they could, then Smith headed up the shallower water in a canoe with two compatriots and two Indian guides.

While Smith was plunging deeper into the wilderness, the seven men on the barge disobeyed his orders and went ashore. Indians attacked and killed them all. Meanwhile, far upriver, Smith left the canoe and ventured inland on foot with one guide. After about 15 minutes he heard "hallowing," and he bound his guide to his arm as a human shield against the expected attack. Overwhelmed, he fought as best he could, killing two Indians, but finally found himself stuck waist-deep in a bog and had to surrender. Both his companions waiting at the canoe were slaughtered. The Indians marched Smith to Opechancanough, brother of Powhatan. A crowd collected around the captor. Showing no fear, Smith calmly pulled his compass from his pocket and demonstrated its workings; the onlookers were amazed. Nevertheless, they tied him to a tree and were ready to shoot him, when Opechancanough stepped in. Smith's language skills no doubt played a part in his survival; one of his fellows, he later learned, had been the victim of a hideous torture ceremony.

For the next several weeks, Smith was moved from village to village. The Indian intelligence network verified that he was an important leader—one of the reasons they kept him alive. Interrogated about the strength of Jamestown, Smith exaggerated—a skill that came naturally to him—predicting harsh reprisal if the fort was attacked. They created a small stir in each Indian village as they went north across the Pamunkey River and as far as the Rappahannock. By this time, he was on friendly terms with his captors and—ever the alert explorer—managed to learn something about the countryside beyond. At the house of one minor chief, he was treated to a startling ceremony when a priest came skipping around the fire. The shaman was painted with coal and oil, stuffed weasel and snakeskins hanging from his head and shoulders. The ensuing feasting and drinking went on for three days.

Eventually Smith was brought before the great chief Powhatan, in Werowocomoco on the Pamunkey (York) River. He was impressed by Powhatan's proud, regal bearing. When the chief asked what the English were up to, Smith improvised, telling him that his men were forced ashore, retreating from the Spanish. He elaborated on the lie, explaining that they had journeyed inland to strike at the Monocans, Powhatan's enemy, in revenge for an earlier attack. Whether Powhatan believed him or simply let the issue go, he then offered to provide Jamestown with meat and corn, as well as protection, in return for trade goods and the promise that the English would relocate downriver from Werowocomoco and acknowledge Powhatan as their ruler. Smith would not agree to this, any more than he would agree to another chief's suggestion that he forsake the settlement and become a local chief, with the accompanying benefits of property and women. He made some bluff, and then a strange ceremony began.

The Indians brought out two stones, dragged Smith to them, placed his head on them, and were on the point of beating out his brains with clubs when the king's daughter, Pocahontas, intervened.

This touching, mythic event did not appear in Smith's first report, written some five months later in June 1608. It was first published in 1624, in his General History. By then Pocahontas had already died. In the intervening years, she had grown from a girl of about 12, to a popular teenage free spirit, wheeling half naked around Jamestown, to a symbol of racial harmony when she married settler John Rolfe. Celebrated in England and received by the king and queen, she died before she could return to America. Smith by then was on his way to becoming one of England's foremost historians. He may have misinterpreted or embellished his memory of the ceremony to include his own fleeting relationship with Pocahontas. Some scholars, believing she would not have questioned her father's decision in front of his cohorts, think the event was some kind of adoption ritual. There is also the possibility that Pocahontas made Smith think she was saving his life so that he would feel himself in debt to Powhatan. More than one scholar, though, has argued that Smith himself is the best judge of what was happening, since he was actually there. At any rate, shortly thereafter, Smith was released.

Powhatan had decided that the English were not a serious threat and could be used to obtain metal and goods. He sent Smith off, exacting from him a promise to return with two big guns and a grindstone. Back at the settlement, Smith must have smiled inwardly at the deal he had struck. As good as his word, he turned over the guns and grindstone to the Indian porters who came along. The guns were demiculverins, small cannons that weighed about two tons each. In a rare instance of understatement, Smith reported that the Indians found them "somewhat too heavy." He demonstrated their power by firing one at an ice-laden tree, and at the shattering explosion the Indians scattered. Smith laughed and called them back, then gave them some trinkets that left them happy. Or so he imagined.

IT MIGHT WELL BE THOUGHT a country so fair (as Virginia is) and a people so tractable would long ere this have been quietly possessed, to the satisfaction of the adventurers, and the eternalizing of the memory of those that effected it. But because all the world do see a defailement [*failure*], this following treatise shall give satisfaction to all indifferent readers, how the business has been carried, where no doubt they will easily understand and answer to their question, how it came to pass there was no better speed and success in those proceedings.

Captain Bartholomew Gosnold, one of the first movers of this plantation [*colony*], having many years solicited many of his friends, but found small assistance, at last prevailed with some gentlemen, as Captain John Smith, Master Edward Maria Wingfield, Master Robert Hunt, and divers [*various*] others, who depended a year upon his projects.

But nothing could be effected, till by their great charge and industry, it came to be apprehended by certain of the nobility, gentry, and merchants, so that his Majesty by his letters patents, gave commission for establishing councils, to direct here, and to govern, and to execute there. To effect this was spent another year, and, by that, three ships were provided—one of 100 tons, another of 40, and a pinnace of 20. [*The* Susan Constant *was actually 120 tons; the smaller vessels were the* Godspeed *and the* Discovery.]

The transportation of the company was committed to Captain Christopher Newport, a mariner well practiced for the western parts of America. But their orders for government were put in a box, not to be opened, nor the governors known until they arrived in Virginia.

On the 19 of December, 1606, we set sail from Blackwall, but by unprosperous winds, were kept six weeks in the sight of England, all which time Master Hunt our preacher was so weak and sick that few expected his recovery. Yet although he were but twenty miles

Smith's route December 1606 – April 1607
□ Colonial settlement with date of founding
● Present-day city
present-day coastlines shown

NORTH AMERICA
EUROPE
Area of main map
Atlantic Ocean
AFRICA
SOUTH AMERICA

ENGLAND
London ●
FRANCE
EUROPE
SPAIN

NORTH AMERICA
□ Plymouth (1620)
Washington
● □ Jamestown (1607)
Roanoke (1584)
Bermuda

ATLANTIC OCEAN

2100 mi/3380 km

Canary Islands

1450 mi/2334 km

West Indies

AFRICA

Caribbean Sea

Enlarged below

3200 mi/5150 km

Route through the West Indies

Isle of Virgins (Virgin Islands)
Anguilla
Puerto Rico
Saba
St. Martin
Isla Mona
St. Croix
St. Eustatius
St. Kitts
Nevis
Antigua
Montserrat
Guadeloupe
Marie-Galante

Caribbean Sea

Dominica

mi 0   100   200
km 0   100   200

Martinique

ATLANTIC OCEAN

mi 0   600   1200
km 0   600   1200

THE ORIGINAL JAMESTOWN COLONISTS' ATLANTIC
CROSSING ROUTE, THROUGH THE WEST INDIES

from his habitation (the time we were in the Downs [*off the coast of southeastern England*]) and notwithstanding the stormy weather, nor the scandalous imputations (of some few, little better than atheists, of the greatest rank amongst us) suggested against him, all this could never force from him so much as a seeming desire to leave the business, but preferred the service of God, in so good a voyage, before any affection to contest with his godless foes, whose disastrous designs (could they have prevailed) had even then overthrown the business, so many discontents did then arise, had he not with the water of patience and his godly exhortations (but chiefly by his true devoted examples) quenched those flames of envy and dissension.

We watered at the Canaries. We traded with the savages at Dominica. Three weeks we spent in refreshing ourselves amongst these West India Isles. In Guadeloupe we found a bath so hot, as in it we boiled pork as well as over the fire. And at a little isle called Monica, we took from the bushes with our hands near two hogsheads full of birds in three or four hours. In Nevis, Mona, and the Virgin Isles, we spent some time, where, with a loathsome beast like a crocodile, called a gwayn [*iguana*], tortoises, pelicans, parrots, and fishes, we daily feasted. Gone from thence in search of Virginia, the company was not a little discomforted, seeing the mariners had three days passed their reckoning and found no land, so that Captain Ratcliffe (captain of the pinnace) rather desired to bear up the helm to return for England than make further search. But God the guider of all good actions, forcing them by an extreme storm to hull [*furl sails and drift*] all night, did drive them by his providence to their desired port, beyond all their expectations, for never any of them had seen that coast.

The first land they made they called Cape Henry [*southern lip of Chesapeake Bay*]; where 30 of them recreating themselves on shore were assaulted by five savages, who hurt two of the English very dangerously.

That night was the box opened, and the orders read, in which Bartholomew Gosnold, John Smith, Edward Wingfield, Christopher Newport, John Ratcliffe, John Martin, and George Kendall were named to be the Council, and to choose a president amongst them for a year, who with the Council should govern. Matters of moment were to be examined by a jury, but determined by the major part of the Council, in which the president had two voices [*votes*].

Until the 13 of May [1607] they sought a place to plant in. Then the Council was sworn. Master Wingfield was chosen president, and an oration made why Captain Smith was not admitted of the Council as the rest.

[*Suspected of mutiny, Smith was placed under arrest. Wingfield, the only member of the Virginia Company on the expedition, was elected colony president shortly after the landing at the site of Jamestown; he denied Smith his rightful place on the Council. But under protest of the colonists, Smith was sworn in on June 10. In the meantime, though technically still under arrest, Smith had already explored up the James with Newport, who recognized Smith's usefulness. On September 10 Wingfield was deposed and later fined 200 pounds for slandering Smith.*]

Now falleth every man to work. The Council contrive the fort; the rest cut down trees to make place to pitch their tents. Some provide clapboard to relade [*reload*] the ships; some make gardens, some nets, etc. The savages often visited us kindly. The president's overweening jealousy [*fear*] would admit no exercise at arms, or fortification, but the boughs of trees cast together in the form of a half moon by the extraordinary pains and diligence of Captain Kendall.

Newport, Smith, and twenty others were sent to discover the head of the river [*the Powhatan, or James*]. By divers small habitations they passed. In six days they arrived at a town called Powhatan, consisting of some twelve houses, pleasantly seated on a hill, before it three fertile isles, about it many of their cornfields. The place is very pleasant and strong by nature. Of this place the prince is called Powhatan [*actually Powhatan's son Parahunt*], and his people Powhatans. To this place the river is navigable, but higher within a mile. By reason of the rocks and isle, there is not passage for a small boat; this they call the falls.

The people in all parts kindly entreated them, till being returned within twenty miles of Jamestown they gave just cause of jealousy [*suspicion*]. But had God not blessed the discoverers otherwise than

Colonists arrive in Virginia and begin building Jamestown
(19th-century woodcut).

those at the fort, there had then been an end of that plantation.
For at the fort, where they arrived the next day, they found 17 men
hurt and a boy slain by the savages. And had it not chanced a cross-
bar shot [*round shot with a spike through the middle*] from the ships
struck down a bough from a tree amongst them, that caused them
to retire, our men had all been slain, being securely all at work and
their arms in dry fats [*storage casks*].

Hereupon the president was contented the fort should be
palisaded, the ordnance mounted, his men armed and exercised.
For many were the assaults and ambushes of the savages, and our
men by their disorderly straggling were often hurt when the savages by the nimbleness of their heels well escaped. What toil we
had, with so small a power to guard our workmen adays, watch all
night, resist our enemies, and effect our business—to relade the
ships, cut down trees, and prepare the ground to plant our corn,
etc.—I refer to the reader's consideration. Six weeks being spent

in this manner, Captain Newport (who was hired only for our transportation) was to return with the ships.

Now Captain Smith, who all this time from their departure from the Canaries was restrained as a prisoner upon the scandalous suggestions of some of the chief (envying his repute)—who feigned he intended to usurp the government, murder the Council, and make himself king—that his confederates were dispersed in all the three ships and that divers of his confederates that revealed it would affirm it. For this he was committed as a prisoner.

Thirteen weeks he remained thus suspected. And by that time the ships should return they pretended out of their commiserations to refer him to the Council in England to receive a check [reprimand], rather than by particulating his designs make him so odious to the world, as to touch his life, or utterly overthrow his reputation. But he so much scorned their charity, and publicly defied the uttermost of their cruelty, he wisely prevented their policies, though he could not suppress their envies. Yet so well he demeaned [behaved] himself in this business [that] all the company did see his innocence and his adversaries' malice, and those suborned to accuse him accused his accusers of subornation. Many untruths were alleged against him, but being so apparently disproved begat a general hatred in the hearts of the company against such unjust commanders that the president was adjudged to give him 200 pounds, so that all he had was seized upon, in part of satisfaction, which Smith presently returned to the store for the general use of the colony.

Many were the mischiefs that daily sprung from their ignorant (yet ambitious) spirits, but the good doctrine and exhortation of our preacher Master Hunt reconciled them and caused Captain Smith to be admitted of the Council.

The next day all received the communion. The day following the savages voluntarily desired peace, and Captain Newport returned for England with news, leaving in Virginia 100 [*colonists*] the 15 of June 1607.

Being thus left to our fortunes, it fortuned that within ten days scarce ten amongst us could either go, or well stand—such extreme weakness and sickness oppressed us.

And thereat none need marvel if they consider the cause and reason, which was this: While the ships stayed, our allowance was somewhat bettered by a daily proportion of biscuit, which the sailors would pilfer to sell, give, or exchange with us for money, sassafras, furs, or love. But when they departed, there remained neither tavern, beer house, nor place of relief but the common kettle. Had we been as free from all sins as [*we were from*] gluttony and drunkenness, we might have been canonized for saints. But our president would never have been admitted [*canonized*] for engrossing to his private oatmeal, sack, oil, aqua vitae, beef, eggs, or whatnot. But the kettle? That indeed he allowed equally to be distributed. And that was half a pint of wheat, and as much barley boiled with water for a man a day—and this (having fried some 26 weeks in the ship's hold) contained as many worms as grains, so that we might truly call it rather so much bran than corn. Our drink was water, our lodgings castles in the air. With this lodging and diet, our extreme toil in bearing and planting palisades, so strained and bruised us, and our continual labor in the extremity of the heat had so weakened us, as were cause sufficient to have made us as miserable in our native country, or any other place in the world.

From May to September, those that escaped [*survived*] lived upon sturgeon and sea crabs. Fifty in this time we buried. The rest seeing the president's projects to escape these miseries in our pinnace by flight (who all this time had neither felt want nor sickness) so moved our dead spirits, as we deposed him and established Ratcliffe in his place (Gosnold being dead, Kendall deposed, Smith newly recovered). With the skillful diligence of Master Thomas

Wotton our surgeon general, Martin and Ratcliffe were by his care preserved and relieved, and the most of the soldiers recovered.

[*Of the seven original Council members, Bartholomew Gosnold became sick on August 1 and died three weeks later. By the end of the summer George Kendall was in prison for "heinous" conduct; he was later convicted of being an informant to the Spanish. Captain Christopher Newport returned to England in June, then came back to Jamestown in January 1608; he would make three more trips to Virginia. Edward Maria Wingfield, as already noted, was deposed in September; he was imprisoned on the pinnace with Kendall, and in April 1608 was returned to England in disgrace. Captain John Martin was often sick. John Smith himself was briefly sick during that first summer. John Ratcliffe (who for some unknown reason used the alias Sicklemore) was thus the only Council member able to assume the presidency in September.*]

But now was all our provision spent, the sturgeon gone, all helps abandoned, each hour expecting the fury of the savages, when God the patron of all good endeavors, in that desperate extremity so changed the hearts of the savages that they brought such plenty of their fruits and provision as no man wanted.

And now where some affirmed it was ill done of the Council to send forth men so badly provided, this uncontradictable reason will show them plainly they are too ill advised to nourish such ill conceits. First, the fault of our going was our own. What could be thought fitting or necessary we had, but what we should find, or want, or where we should be, we were all ignorant. And supposing to make our passage in two months—with victuals to live, and the advantage of the spring to work—we were at sea five months, where we both spent our victuals and lost the opportunity of the time and season to plant, by the unskillful presumption of our ignorant transporters that understood not at all what they undertook.

Such actions have ever since the world's beginning been subject to such accidents, and everything of worth is found full of difficulties. But nothing [is] so difficult as to establish a commonwealth so far remote from men and means and where men's minds are so untoward as neither do well themselves nor suffer others. But to proceed:

The new president and Martin, being little beloved, of weak judgment in dangers, and less industry in peace, committed the managing of all things abroad to Captain Smith [*Smith became the supply officer*], who by his own example, good words, and fair promises, set some to mow, others to bind thatch, some to build houses, others to thatch them, himself always bearing the greatest task for his own share. So that in short time he provided most of them lodgings, neglecting any for himself.

This done, seeing the savages' superfluity begin to decrease (with some of his workmen), shipped himself in the shallop [*a small open boat*] to search the country for trade. The want of the language, knowledge to manage his boat without sails [*sailors*], the want of a sufficient power (knowing the multitude of the savages), apparel for his men, and other necessaries, were infinite impediments, yet no discouragement.

Being but six or seven in company, he went down the river to Kecoughtan [*mouth of the James, northern side*], where at first they scorned him as a famished man, and would in derision offer him a handful of corn, a piece of bread, for their swords and muskets, and suchlike proportions also for their apparel. But seeing by trade and courtesy there was nothing to be had, he made bold to try such conclusions [*experiments*] as necessity enforced, though contrary to his commission: let fly his muskets, ran his boat on shore, whereat they all fled into the woods. So marching toward their houses, they might see great heaps of corn—much ado he had to restrain his hungry soldiers from present taking of it, expecting as it happened that the savages would assault them, as not long after they did with a most hideous noise. Sixty or seventy of them, some black, some red, some white, some parti-colored, came in a square order, singing and dancing out of the woods, with their *Okee* (which was an idol made of skins, stuffed with moss, all painted and hung with chains and copper) borne before them. And in this manner, being well armed with clubs, targets [*shields*], bows, and arrows, they charged the English, that so kindly received them with their muskets loaded with pistol shot that down fell their god, and divers lay sprawling on the ground. The rest fled again to the woods, and ere long sent one of their *quiyoughcosughes* [*high priests*] to offer peace, and redeem their *Okee*. Smith told them if only six of them would come unarmed and load his boat, he would not only be their friend but restore them their *Okee*, and give them beads, copper, and hatchets besides— which on both sides was to their contents performed. And then they brought him venison, turkeys, wild fowl, bread, and what they had, singing and dancing in sign of friendship till they departed. In his return he discovered the town and country of Warraskoyack.

> Thus God unboundless by his power,
> Made them thus kind would us devour.

Smith, perceiving (notwithstanding their late misery) not any regarded but from hand to mouth (the company being well recovered), caused the pinnace to be provided with things fitting to get provision for the year following. But in the interim he made three or four journeys and discovered the people of Chickahominy. Yet what he carefully provided, the rest carelessly spent.

Wingfield and Kendall, living in disgrace, seeing all things at random in the absence of Smith, the company's dislike of their president's weakness, and their small love to Martin's never mending sickness, strengthened themselves with the sailors and other confederates to regain their former credit and authority—or at least such means aboard the pinnace (being fitted to sail as Smith had appointed for trade) to alter her course and to go for England.

Smith, unexpectedly returning, had the plot discovered to him. Much trouble he had to prevent it, till with store of sakre [*a cannon*] and musket shot he forced them stay or sink in the river, which action cost the life of Captain Kendall. These brawls are so disgusting as some will say they were better forgotten, yet all men of good judgment will conclude it were better their baseness should be manifest to the world than the business bear the scorn and shame of their excused disorders. The president and Captain Archer not long after intended also to have abandoned the country, which project also was curbed and suppressed by Smith.

The Spaniard never more greedily desired gold than he [*Smith*] victual, nor his soldiers more to abandon the country than he to keep it. But finding [*he found*] plenty of corn in the river of Chickahominy, where hundreds of savages in divers places stood with baskets expecting his coming. And now the winter approaching, the rivers became so covered with swans, geese, ducks, and cranes, that we daily feasted with good bread, Virginia peas, pumpkins, and persimmons, fish, fowl, and diverse sorts of wild beasts as fat as we could eat them, so that none of our tuftaffaty humorists [*charlatans dressed in tufted taffeta*] desired to go for England.

But our comedies never endured long without a tragedy. Some idle exceptions being muttered against Captain Smith for not discovering the head of Chickahominy River (and taxed by the Council to be too slow in so worthy an attempt), the next voyage he proceeded so far that with much labor by cutting of trees in sunder he made his passage. But when his barge could pass no farther, he left her in a broad bay out of danger of shot, commanding none should go ashore till his return. Himself with two English and two savages went up higher in a canoe, but he was not long absent.

Their triumph about him

C: S

C: Smith bound to a tree to be shott to death
1607

PAMUNKEYS TRIUMPH OVER SMITH (DETAIL FROM
ILLUSTRATION IN 1624 *GENERAL HISTORY*).

But his men went ashore, whose want of government gave both
occasion and opportunity to the savages to surprise one George Cassen, whom they slew, and much failed not to have cut off the boat
and all the rest. When he [*Powhatan*] would punish any notorious

enemy or malefactor, he causes him to be tied to a tree, and with mussel shells or reeds the executioner cuts off his joints one after another, ever casting what they cut off into the fire. Then doth he proceed with shells and reeds to case the skin from his head and face. Then do they rip his belly and so burn him with the tree and all. Thus themselves reported they executed George Cassen.

Smith little dreaming of that accident, being got to the marshes at the river's head 20 miles in the desert, had his two men slain (as is supposed) sleeping by the canoe, whilst himself by fowling sought them victual, who finding he was beset with 200 savages, two of them he slew, still defending himself with the aid of a savage his guide, whom he bound to his arm with his garters and used him as a buckler [shield]. Yet he was shot in his thigh a little, and had many arrows that stuck in his clothes but no great hurt. Till at last, slipping into a bogmire, they took him prisoner.

When this news came to Jamestown, much was their sorrow for his loss, few expecting what ensued. Six or seven weeks [closer to three weeks, from about December 10, 1607 to January 1, 1608] those barbarians kept him prisoner. Many strange triumphs and conjurations they made of him, yet he so demeaned [behaved] himself amongst them, as he not only diverted them from surprising the fort but procured his own liberty, and got himself and his company such estimation amongst them that those savages admired him more than their own quiyoughcosughes. The manner how they used and delivered him, is as follows.

The savages having drawn from George Cassen whether Captain Smith was gone, prosecuting that opportunity they followed him with 300 bowmen, conducted by the king of Pamunkey [Opechancanough, Powhatan's half-brother], who in divisions searching the turnings of the river, found Robinson and Emry by the fireside. Those they shot full of arrows and slew. Then finding the captain, as is said, that used the savage that was his guide as his shield (three of them being slain and divers others so galled), all the rest would not come near him. Thinking thus to have returned to his boat, regarding them as he marched more than his way, [he] slipped up to the middle in an oozy creek and his savage with him. Yet dared they not come to him till being near dead with cold, he threw away his arms. Then according to their composition [agreement], they drew him forth and led him to the fire, where his men were slain. Diligently they chafed [massaged] his benumbed limbs.

He demanding for their captain, they showed him Opechancanough, to whom he gave a round, ivory, double compass dial. Much they marveled at the playing of the fly and needle, which they could see so plainly, and yet not touch it because of the glass that covered them. But when he demonstrated by that globe-like jewel the roundness of the earth and skies, the sphere of the sun, moon, and stars, and how the sun did chase the night round about the world continually, the greatness of the land and sea, the diversity of nations, variety of complexions, and how we were to them antipodes, and many other suchlike matters, they all stood as amazed with admiration. Notwithstanding, within an hour after, they tied him to a tree, and as many as could stand about him prepared to shoot him. But the king holding up the compass in his hand, they all laid down their bows and arrows, and in a triumphant manner led him to Orapaks [a hunting village], where he was after their manner kindly feasted and well used.

[Smith's careful observations during his captivity and other times rank him as the foremost source on Chesapeake Indian ethnology. The following passages indicate his heightened state of awareness.]

Their order in conducting him was thus: Drawing themselves all in file, the king in the midst had all their pieces and swords borne before him. Captain Smith was led after him by three great

CONJURATION CEREMONY WITH SMITH IN FOREGROUND
(*GENERAL HISTORY*, 1624)

savages, holding him fast by each arm. And on each side six went
in file with their arrows nocked. But arriving at the town (which
was but only 30 or 40 hunting houses made of mats, which they
remove as they please, as we our tents) all the women and children staring to behold him, the soldiers first all in file performed
the form of a bisonn   *rbour calls this a snakelike troop maneuver,
from the Italian bi*   *rge snake]* so well as could be, and
on each flank o*   *s to see them keep their order.

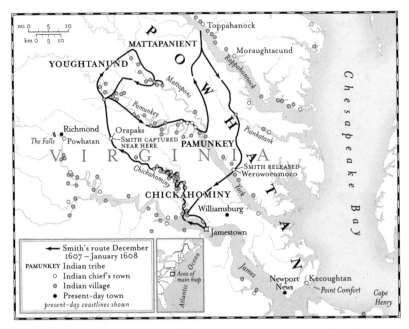

APPROXIMATE ROUTE SMITH TRAVELED AS A PRISONER
OF THE PAMUNKEYS

A good time they continued this exercise, and then cast themselves in a ring, dancing in such several postures and singing
and yelling out such hellish notes and screeches, being strangely
painted, every one his quiver of arrows and at his back a club,
on his arm a fox or an otter's skin, or some such matter for his
vambrace [*forearm armor*]. Their heads and shoulders painted red,
with oil and *pocones* [*puccoon root, a red vegetable dye*] mingled together, which scarlet-like color made an exceedingly handsome
show—his bow in his hand and the skin of a bird with her wings
abroad dried, tied on his head, a piece of copper, a white shell,
a long feather, with a small rattle growing at the tails of their
snakes tied to it, or some suchlike toy. All this while Smith and
the king stood in the midst guarded, as before is said, and after
three dances they all departed.

Smith they conducted to a longhouse, where thirty or forty tall fellows did guard him, and ere long more bread and venison was brought him than would have served twenty men. I think his stomach at that time was not very good; what he left they put in baskets and tied over his head. About midnight they set the meat again before him. All this time not one of them would eat a bite with him, till the next morning they brought him as much more, and then did they eat all the old and reserved the new as they had done the other, which made him think they would fat him to eat him. Yet in this desperate estate to defend him from the cold, one Maocassater brought him his gown, in requital of some beads and toys Smith had given him at his first arrival in Virginia.

Two days after, a man would have slain him (but that the guard prevented it) for the death of his son, to whom they conducted him to recover [restore] the poor man—then breathing his last. Smith told them that at Jamestown he had a water [medicine] would do it, if they would let him fetch it, but they would not permit that but made all the preparations they could to assault Jamestown, craving his advice. And for recompense he should have life, liberty, land, and women. In part of a table book [tablet] he wrote his mind to them at the fort: what was intended, how they should follow that direction to affright the messengers, and without fail send him such things as he wrote for, and an inventory with them. He told the savages of the mines, great guns, and other engines, [which] exceedingly affrighted them. Yet according to his request they went to Jamestown in as bitter weather as could be of frost and snow, and within three days returned with an answer.

But when they came to Jamestown, seeing men sally out as he had told them they would, they fled. Yet in the night they came again to the same place where he had told them they should receive an answer, and such things as he had promised them, which they found accordingly, and with which they returned with no small expedition, to the wonder of them all that heard it, that he could either divine, or the paper could speak [the Indians had no writing]. Then they led him to the Youghtanunds, the Mattapanients, the Piankatanks, the Nantaughtacunds, and Onawmanients upon the rivers of Rappahannock and Patawomeck [Potomac]—over all those rivers and back again by divers other several nations, to the king's habitation at Pamunkey, where they entertained him with most strange and fearful conjurations.

As if near led to hell,
Amongst the devils to dwell.
—Seneca

Not long after, early in a morning a great fire was made in a longhouse, and a mat spread on the one side as on the other. On the one they caused him to sit, and all the guard went out of the house and presently came skipping in a great grim fellow, all painted over with coal mingled with oil, and many snakes and weasels' skins stuffed with moss and all their tails tied together, so as they met on the crown of his head in a tassel. And round about the tassel was as a coronet of feathers, the skins hanging round about his head, back, and shoulders, and in a manner covered his face. With a hellish voice and a rattle in his hand, with most strange gestures and passions, he began his invocation, and environed the fire with a circle of meal. Which done, three more suchlike devils came rushing in with the like antic tricks, painted half black, half red. But all their eyes were painted white, and some red strokes like mustaches along their cheeks. Round about him those fiends danced a pretty while, and then came in three more as ugly as the rest, with red eyes and white strokes over their black faces.

At last they all sat down right against him—three of them on the one hand of the chief priest, and three on the other. Then all with their rattles began a song; which ended, the chief priest laid down five wheat corns. Then straining his arms and hands with such violence that he sweated and his veins swelled, he began a short oration. At the conclusion they all gave a short groan, and then laid down three grains more. After that, began their song again, and then another oration, ever laying down so many corns as before, till they had twice encircled the fire. That done, they took a bunch of little sticks prepared for that purpose, continuing still their devotion, and at the end of every song and oration, they laid down a stick betwixt the divisions of corn. Till night, neither he nor they did either eat or drink. And then they feasted merrily, with the best provisions they could make.

Three days they used this ceremony, the meaning whereof, they told him, was to know if he intended them well or no. The circle of meal signified their country, the circles of corn the bounds of the sea, and the sticks his country. They imagined the world to be flat and round, like a trencher, and they in the middest. After this they brought him a [his] bag of gunpowder, which they carefully preserved till the next spring, to plant as they did their corn, because they would be acquainted with the nature of that seed.

Opitchapam, the king's brother, invited him to his house, where, with as many platters of bread, fowl, and wild beasts as did environ him, he bid him welcome. But not any of them would eat a bite with him, but put up all the remainder in baskets. At his return to Opechancanough's, all the king's women and their children flocked about him for their parts, as a due by custom, to be merry with such fragments.

At last they brought him to Werowocomoco, where was Powhatan their emperor. Here more than two hundred of those grim

King Powhatan comands C.Smith to be slayne, his daughter Pokahontas beggs his life his thankfull and how he subiected 30 of their kings, read the

POCAHONTAS SAVES SMITH'S LIFE AFTER POWHATAN
COMMANDS HIM "TO BE SLAIN" (*GENERAL HISTORY,* 1624).

courtiers stood wondering at him, as he had been a monster, till Powhatan and his train had put themselves in their greatest braveries.

Before a fire, upon a seat like a bedstead, he sat covered with a great robe made of raccoon skins, and all the tails hanging by.

On either hand did sit a young wench of sixteen or eighteen years, and along on each side the house, two rows of men, and behind them as many women with all their heads and shoulders painted red. Many of their heads [were] bedecked with the white down of birds, but everyone with something, and a great chain of white beads about their necks.

At his entrance before the king, all the people gave a great shout. The queen of Appomattoc was appointed to bring him water to wash his hands, and another brought him a bunch of feathers instead of a towel to dry them.

He kindly welcomed me with good words and great platters of sundry victuals, assuring me his friendship and my liberty within four days. He asked me the cause of our coming. I told him, being in fight with the Spaniards our enemy, being overpowered, near put to retreat, and by extreme weather put to this shore, where landing at Chesapeake the people shot [at] us. But at Kecoughtan they kindly used us. We by signs demanded fresh water; they described us up the river was all fresh water. At Paspahegh [near Jamestown] also they kindly used us. Our pinnace being leaky we were forced to stay to mend her till Captain Newport, my father, came to conduct us away.

He demanded why we went further with our boat. I told him, in that I would have occasion to talk of the back sea, that on the other side [of] the main, where was salt water, my father had a child slain, which we supposed Monacan his enemy had done, whose death we intended to revenge.

After good deliberation, he began to describe me the countries beyond the falls, with many of the rest, confirming what not only Opechancanough and an Indian which had been prisoner to Powhatan had before told me, but some called it five days, some six, some eight, where the said water dashed amongst many stones and rocks, each storm which caused oft times the head of the river to be brackish. Atquanachuke he described to be the people that had slain my brother, whose death he would revenge. He described also upon the same sea a mighty nation called Pocoughtaonack, a fierce nation that did eat men, and warred with the people of Moyaones and Patawomeck [Potomac], nations upon the top of the head of the bay, under his territories, where the year before they had slain a hundred. He signified their crowns were shaven, long hair in the neck, tied [in] a knot, swords like poleaxes. Beyond them he described people with short coats and sleeves to the elbows that passed that way in ships like ours. Many kingdoms he described me to the head of the bay, which seemed to be a mighty river, issuing from mighty mountains betwixt the two seas. [The previous three paragraphs are from A True Relation, Barbour, Vol. I, pp. 53-55.]

Having feasted him after their best barbarous manner they could, a long consultation was held. But the conclusion was two great stones were brought before Powhatan. Then as many as could laid hands on him [Smith], dragged him to them, and thereon laid his head. And being ready with their clubs to beat out his brains, Pocahontas, the king's dearest daughter, when no entreaty could prevail, got his head in her arms, and laid her own upon his to save him from death.

Whereat the emperor was contented he should live to make him hatchets, and her bells, beads, and copper. For they thought him as well of all occupations as themselves. For the king himself will make his own robes, shoes, bows, arrows, pots; plant, hunt, or do anything so well as the rest.

Two days after, Powhatan, having disguised himself in the most fearful manner he could, caused Captain Smith to be brought forth to a great house in the woods, and there upon a mat by the fire to be left alone. Not long after, from behind a mat that divided the house, was made the most doleful noise he ever heard. Then Powhatan more like a devil than a man—with some two hundred more as black as himself— came unto him and told him now they were friends, and presently he [Smith] should go to Jamestown to send him two great guns and a grindstone, for which he would give him the country of Capahowasic and forever esteem him as his son Nantaquoud.

So to Jamestown with twelve guides Powhatan sent him. That night they quartered in the woods, he still expecting (as he had done all this long time of his imprisonment) every hour to be put to one death or other, for all their feasting. But almighty God (by his divine providence) had mollified the hearts of those stern barbarians with compassion.

The next morning betimes they came to the fort, where Smith having used the savages with what kindness he could, he showed Rawhunt, Powhatan's trusty servant, two demiculverins and a millstone to carry Powhatan. They found them somewhat too heavy. But when they did see him discharge them, being loaded with stones, among the boughs of a great tree loaded with icicles, the ice and branches came so tumbling down that the poor savages ran away half dead with fear. But at last we regained some conference with them, and gave them such toys, and sent to Powhatan, his women, and children such presents as gave them in general full content.

CHAPTER TWO

Smith Becomes a Werowance

January 2 to June 1, 1608

SMITH THE MIRACLE SURVIVOR *was for the most part welcomed back to Jamestown. The leaders, however, felt a bit differently about their wayward fellow councillor. They sentenced him to death for the loss of his men. Smith had enough clout by then to refuse to comply, and by sheer luck his old ally, Captain Newport, returned from England with a shipload of new recruits the very next day, January 2, 1608.*

Newport had left the colony back in the summer when things were still looking fine. Little did he know the toll that disease and starvation had taken. As though in punishment for their dreams of easy plunder, winter had struck the colony with a vengeance. An especially hard frost hit during the 1607-08 season, cold and frostbite adding to the settlers' miseries. The newcomers (the "first supply"), buoyed by Newport's positive reports, were shocked by the pitiful condition of Jamestown that winter. When spring finally came, only 38 of the original 105 colonists were still living. Since Newport's departure, nearly two-thirds of the colony had perished, the council president had been deposed and was under arrest, another councillor had been shot, and yet another (Smith) had just been sentenced to death. Nothing of worth had been discovered or produced, and the gentry were in favor of abandoning the colony.

Desperate for a breakthough, Smith and Newport knew that something of lasting value had to be found soon, or the Virginia Company might pull out. Gold mines beyond the mountains were still a possibility. Among the new arrivals were 33 gentlemen, 21 laborers, 6 tailors, 2 apothecaries, a gunsmith, a blacksmith, a tobacco-pipe maker, a perfumer, and—reflecting the company's steady optimism—2 refiners and 2 goldsmiths.

Smith was the crucial link, the most savvy and skilled negotiator. The Indians preferred dealing with him, though they also, at Smith's urging, recognized Newport as a white leader. From this point on, Smith's stock began to rise—he knew the countryside and the natives better than anyone in Jamestown, and he had arguably saved it from annihilation during his captivity. More and more, the settlers began looking to him as an authoritative leader whose strength and experience could help them succeed.

Smith, Newport, and a retinue of some 40 guards set off down the James, up around the Virginia Peninsula, and then up the York River to Werowocomoco to pay a visit to Powhatan. As the eagle flies, Jamestown was less than 20 miles southwest of Powhatan's village, but through a forbidding, swampy wilderness. Thus the 100 miles by water was the only reasonable way to travel with a large armed contingent.

While Newport stayed back on the river in case of ambush, Smith went ahead with half the men. Hundreds of people turned out, dressed in their best, to greet the white men. Powhatan reminded Smith that he still owed him some guns, yet had to laugh when Smith told him what had happened. Next time, he told Smith, send "some of less burthen." Then Smith requested the lands and provisions Powhatan had promised. Powhatan countered by requesting that Smith's men lay down their arms. Never one to be outpositioned in a deal, Smith replied that the request was "a ceremony our enemies desired, but never our friends." Instead, Smith offered as a pledge that they should exchange young men: Each side would hold someone from the other side in a kind of cultural exchange—in reality a security deposit. The English presented a 13-year-old with the apt name of Thomas Savage, whose trusting spirit of adventure must have been high. In return, the Indians sent over a servant named Namontack.

Powhatan was pleased with the arrangement; he pronounced Smith a werowance, or chief, and declared all the settlers members of the Powhatan community. Smith's critics would later use this against him, saying he was plotting to set up a kingdom and rule with Powhatan as his ally. Such were the suspicions of those with little knowledge of the local language and thus limited interaction with the leaders.

The next day the trading began. Powhatan took charge, sternly asking Newport why his men were armed. He then demanded that Newport in effect show his hand—bring out all the English copper and hatchets before he would decide how much corn to pay. Smith advised against this "ancient trick" to reduce the value of the trade goods, yet Newport complied with the chief. Smith was now annoyed that Powhatan had gained a subtle strategic advantage over them, not only in the price of the corn, but in taking the measure of his trading partners. Newport reasoned that the diplomatic thing to do was make a quick sale and then hope that the friendly exchange would help the English locate the gold that much more quickly. Smith, on the other hand, had a different, longer term outlook—the future of the colony depended, he felt, on maintaining strength in all their relations with the Indians. An old hand at this kind of haggling, Smith managed to buy hundreds of bushels of corn for a few pounds of beads by arguing that they were a rare gem worn only by the greatest royalty in Europe.

But before the colony had a chance to breathe a sigh of relief, a new calamity hit. A devastating fire swept through Jamestown, destroying the storehouse, houses, church, and kitchen. Most of the reserve supplies suddenly went up in flames. With no food and nothing to shield them from the cold, the settlers had to depend again upon the mercy of the Indians.

On April 10, 1608, Newport departed again for England, laden with "ore." Smith escorted him in the pinnace—the smallest of the three original ships—up to the capes at the river's mouth. On his return he took time out to explore the Nansemond River, on the south side of the James. Sailing as far upriver as the 50-foot-long boat would go, he and his crew found a land "so sweet, so pleasant, so beautiful, and so strong a prospect for an invincible strong city, with so many commodities, that I know as yet I have not seen." History has proved the prediction almost but not quite right, the area now an exurban extension of Portsmouth.

Back at the settlement Indian trouble was brewing. People working outside the fort were continually being harassed by thieves who coveted the settlers' tools. One day when Smith and a companion were working a cornfield, two Indians threatened to thrash them. They followed Smith back inside the fort and were promptly arrested along with some other Indians milling about. Smith was ordered to pump them for information about a possible plot against the fort and to torture them if they wouldn't speak. The English also threatened to hang the captives if all the stolen tools were not returned. One Indian confessed that there was indeed a plan to ambush Newport on his return and then attack the fort. Whether or not his story was accurate, it underscored the settlers' need to strive for self-sufficiency and to remain on the alert outside the fort. The arrival of another boatload of settlers later that spring helped bolster morale.

Around this time Ratcliffe floated the idea of leading an expedition inland to search for gold above the rivers' fall line. Smith opposed the plan, saying that more "gilded dirt" was a waste of time, when they could be sending back cedar and other such prevalent resources. No doubt he already had in mind leading a similar outing, in which he himself would take the credit for any discoveries. At any rate, Ratcliffe's plan was shot down by the Council on the grounds that Newport was the proper one to undertake such a trip.

Despite what he had said against Ratcliffe's proposal, it was not long before Smith offered to lead an expedition himself. On his last visit to Powhatan, the chief had showed Smith the big canoes his people used for rowing to the eastern shore. Intrigued with what might lie up there, and ever hopeful of further clues to finding gold and a navigable route to the

Pacific, Smith convinced the Council to let him lead an expedition up
the bay. At the very least he would learn priceless information about the
locals, the resources, and the possibilities for trade and alliances. Here was
a chance for real lasting glory, and Smith jumped on it.

Now in Jamestown they were all in combustion, the strongest
preparing once more to run away with the pinnace; which with
the hazard of his life, with sakre falcon [*light ordinance*] and musket
shot, Smith forced [*them*] now the third time to stay or sink. Some
no better than they should be had plotted with the president the
next day to have put him to death by the Levitical law, for the lives
of Robinson and Emry, pretending the fault was his that had led
them to their ends. But he quickly took such order with such law-
yers that he laid them by the heels till he sent some of them prisoners for England [*possibly Smith's exaggeration*]. Now every once in
four or five days, Pocahontas with her attendants brought him so
much provision that saved many of their lives, that else for all this
had starved with hunger.

His relation of the plenty he had seen, especially at Werowocomoco, and of the state and bounty of Powhatan (which till that
time was unknown), so revived their dead spirits, especially the
love of Pocahontas, as all men's fear was abandoned. Thus you may
see what difficulties still crossed any good endeavor. And the good
success of the business being thus often brought to the very period of destruction, yet you see by what strange means God has
still delivered it. As for the insufficiency of them admitted in commission, that error could not be prevented by the electors, there
being no other choice, and all strangers to each other's education,
qualities, or disposition.

And if any deem it a shame to our nation to have any mention made of those enormities, let them peruse the histories of the
Spaniards' discoveries and plantations, where they may see how

many mutinies, disorders, and dissensions have accompanied them and crossed their attempts.

Now whether it had been better for Captain Smith to have concluded with any of those several projects, to have abandoned the country with some ten or twelve of them who were called the better sort, and have left Master Hunt our preacher, Master Anthony Gosnold [Bartholomew's brother], a most honest, worthy, and industrious gentleman, Master Thomas Wotton, and some twenty-seven others of his countrymen to the fury of the savages, famine, and all manner of mischiefs and inconveniences (for they were but forty in all to keep possession of this large country), or starve himself with them for company for want of lodging, or but adventuring abroad to make them provision, or by his opposition to preserve the action and save all their lives, I leave to the censure of all honest men to consider.

All this time our care was not so much to abandon the country but [if] the treasurer and Council in England were as diligent and careful to supply us. Two good ships they sent us, with near a hundred men, well furnished with all things could be imagined necessary, both for them and us, the one commanded by Captain Newport, the other by Captain Francis Nelson, an honest man and an expert mariner. But such was the leewardness of his ship that, though he was within the sight of Cape Henry, by stormy contrary winds was he forced so far to sea that the West Indies was the next land for the repair of his masts and relief of wood and water.

But Newport got in and arrived at Jamestown not long after the redemption of Captain Smith, to whom the savages, as is said, every other day repaired with such provisions that sufficiently did serve them from hand to mouth. Part always they brought him as presents from their kings or Pocahontas; the rest he as their market clerk set the price himself, how they should sell. So he had enchanted these poor souls being their prisoner! And now Newport, whom he called his "father," arriving near as directly as he foretold,

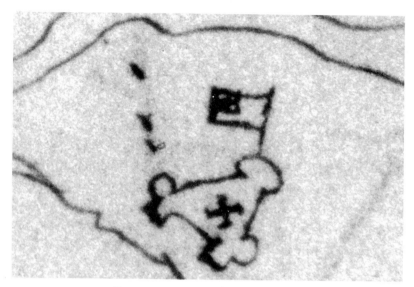

JAMESTOWN FORT (DETAIL FROM
SMITH'S SKETCH MAP OF 1608)

they esteemed him as an oracle, and had them at that submission
he might command them what he listed. That God that created all
things they knew he adored for his god they would also in their
discourses term the god of Captain Smith.

But the president and Council so much envied his estimation
among the savages (though we all in general equally participated
with him of the good thereof), that they wrought it into the savages'
understandings—by their great bounty in giving four times more
for their commodities than Smith appointed—that their greatness
and authority as much exceeded his as their bounty and liberality.

Now the arrival of this first supply [of colonists] so overjoyed us
that we could not devise too much to please the mariners. We gave
them liberty to truck or trade at their pleasures. But in a short time
it followed that could not be had for a pound of copper, which before was sold us for an ounce. Thus ambition and sufferance cut the
throat of our trade, but confirmed their opinion of the greatness

of Captain Newport (wherewith Smith had possessed Powhatan), especially by the great presents Newport often sent him before he could prepare the pinnace to go and visit him, so that this great savage desired also to see him.

A great coil [*turmoil*] there was to set him forward. When he went he was accompanied with Captain Smith and Master Scrivener, a very wise understanding gentleman, newly arrived and admitted of the Council, with thirty or forty chosen men for their guard. Arriving at Werowocomoco, Newport's conceit of this great savage bred many doubts and suspicions of treacheries, which Smith to make appear was needless, with twenty men well appointed, undertook to encounter the worst that could happen.

Gentlemen
Nathaniel Powell
John Taverner
Robert Behethland
William Dyer
Michael Phettiplace
Thomas Coe
William Phettiplace
Thomas Hope
Anthony Gosnold
Anas Todkill
Richard Wiffin

These, with nine others (whose names I have forgotten) coming ashore, landed amongst a many of creeks, over which they were to pass such poor bridges, only made of a few cratches [*wooden frames*] thrust in the ooze, and three or four poles laid on them, and at the end of them the like, tied together only with barks of trees, that it made them much suspect those bridges were but traps. Which caused Smith to make diverse savages go over first, keeping some of the chief as hostage till half his men was passed, to make a guard for himself and the rest.

But finding all things well, by two or three hundred savages they were kindly conducted to their town, where Powhatan strained himself to the utmost of his greatness to entertain them with great shouts of joy, orations of protestations, and with the most plenty of victuals he could provide to feast them. Sitting upon his bed of mats, his pillow of leather embroidered (after their rude manner with pearl and white beads), his attire a fair robe of skins as large as an Irish mantle, at his head and feet [was] a handsome young woman. On each side [of] his house sat twenty of his concubines, their heads and shoulders painted red, with a great chain of white beads about each of their necks. Before those sat his chief men in like order in his arbor-like house, and more than forty [Indians with] platters of fine bread stood as a guard in two files on each side the door. Four or five hundred people made a guard behind them for our passage; and proclamation was made, none upon pain of death to presume to do us any wrong or discourtesy.

With many pretty discourses to renew their old acquaintance, this great king and our captain spent the time, till the ebb left our barge aground. Then renewing their feasts with feats, dancing, and singing, and suchlike mirth, we quartered that night with Powhatan.

The next day Newport came ashore and received as much content as those people could give him. A boy named Thomas Savage was then given unto Powhatan, whom Newport called his son, for whom Powhatan gave him Namontack, his trusty servant and one of a shrewd, subtle capacity. Three or four days more we spent in feasting, dancing, and trading, wherein Powhatan carried himself so proudly yet discreetly (in his savage manner) as made us all admire his natural gifts, considering his education. As scorning to trade as his subjects did, he bespake Newport in this manner:

"Captain Newport, it is not agreeable to my greatness, in this peddling manner to trade for trifles. And I esteem you also a great werowance. Therefore lay me down all your commodities together. What I like I will take, and in recompense give you what I think fitting their value."

Captain Smith being our interpreter, regarding Newport as his father, knowing best the disposition of Powhatan, told us his intent was but only to cheat us. Yet Captain Newport, thinking to outbrave this savage in ostentation of greatness, and so to bewitch him with his bounty as to have what he listed, it so happened that Powhatan, having his desire, valued his corn at such a rate that I think it better cheap in Spain. For we had not four bushels for that we expected to have twenty hogsheads.

This bred some unkindness between our two captains—Newport seeking to please the unsatiable desire of the savage, Smith to cause the savage to please him. But smothering his distaste to avoid the savage's suspicion, [Smith] glanced [flashed] in the eyes of Powhatan many trifles, who fixed his humor upon a few blue beads. A long time he importunately desired them, but Smith seemed so much the more to affect them, as being composed of a most rare substance of the color of the skies, and not to be worn but by the greatest kings in the world. This made him half mad to be the owner of such strange jewels, so that ere we departed, for a pound or two of blue beads, he brought over my king for 200 or 300 bushels of corn—yet parted good friends.

The like entertainment we found of Opechancanough, king of Pamunkey, whom also he in like manner fitted (at the like rates) with blue beads, which grew by this means, of that estimation, that none durst wear any of them but their great kings, their wives, and children.

And so we returned all well to Jamestown, where this new supply being lodged with the rest, accidentally fired their quarters and so the town, which being but thatched with reeds, the fire was so fierce as it burnt their palisades (though eight or ten yards distant) with their arms, bedding, apparel, and much private provision.

Good Master Hunt our preacher lost all his library and all he had but the clothes on his back, yet none never heard him repine at his loss. This happened in the winter in that extreme frost, 1607.

Now though we had victual sufficient—I mean only of oatmeal, meal, and corn—yet the ship staying fourteen weeks when she might as well have been gone in fourteen days, spent a great part of that [provisions], and near all the rest that was sent to be landed. When they departed, what their discretion could spare us (a little poor meal or two) we called feasts to relish our mouths. Of each somewhat they left us, yet I must confess those that had either money, spare clothes, credit to give bills of payment, gold rings, furs, or any such commodities were ever welcome to this removing tavern. Such was our patience to obey such vile commanders, and buy our own provisions at fifteen times the value, suffering them feast (we bearing the charge) yet must not repine, but fast, lest we should incur the censure of factious and seditious persons. And then leakage, ship rats, and other casualties occasioned them loss, but the vessels and remnants we were glad to receive with all our hearts to make up the account, highly commending their providence for preserving that, lest they should discourage any more to come to us.

Now for all this plenty our ordinary was but meal and water, so that this great charge little relieved our wants, whereby with the extremity of the bitter cold frost and those defects, more than half of us died. I cannot deny but both Smith and Scrivener did their best to amend what was amiss, but with the president went the major part, that their horns were too short [Smith and Scrivener didn't have the authority to order a fairer distribution of the food].

But the worst was our gilded refiners with their golden promises made all men their slaves in hope of recompenses. There was no talk, no hope, no work, but dig gold, wash gold, refine gold, load gold. Such a bruit [noise] of gold, that one mad fellow desired to be buried in the sands lest they should by their art make gold of his bones. Little need there was and less reason the ship should stay, their wages run on, our victuals consume [in] fourteen weeks, that the mariners might say they did help to build such a golden church that we can say the rain washed near to nothing in fourteen days.

Were it that Captain Smith would not applaud all those golden inventions, because they admitted him not to the sight of their trials nor golden consultations, I know not; but I have heard him oft question with Captain Martin and tell him, except he could show him a more substantial trial [assay for gold], he was not enamored with their dirty skill [Smith often leavens his scorn with puns]. Breathing out these and many other passions, never anything did more torment him than to see all necessary business neglected, to fraught such a drunken ship with so much gilded dirt.

Till then we never accounted Captain Newport a refiner, who being ready to set sail for England, and we not having any use of parliaments, plays, petitions, admirals, recorders, interpreters, chronologers, courts of plea, nor justices of peace, sent Master Wingfield and Captain Archer home with him, that had engrossed all those titles, to seek some better place of employment.

The authority now consisting in Captain Martin, and the still sickly president [Ratcliffe], the sale of the store's commodities maintained his estate, as an inheritable revenue. [Clearly Smith was disgusted with these two leaders.]

The spring approaching, and the ship departing, Master Scrivener and Captain Smith divided betwixt them the rebuilding Jamestown: the repairing our palisades; the cutting down trees, preparing our fields, planting our corn, and to rebuild our church and recover our storehouse. All men thus busy at their several labors, Master Nelson arrived with his lost Phoenix. Lost, I say, for that we all deemed him lost. Landing safely all his men (so well he had managed his ill hap), causing the Indian Isles to feed his company, that his victual [added] to that we had gotten, as is said before, was near after our allowance sufficient for half a year. He had not anything but he freely imparted it, which honest dealing (being a mariner) caused us admire him. We would not have wished more than he did for us.

Now to relade this ship with some good tidings, the president (not holding it stood with the dignity of his place to leave the fort) gave order to Captain Smith to discover and search the commodities of the Monacans' country beyond the falls. Sixty able men was allotted them, the which within six days Smith had so well trained to their arms and orders that they little feared with whom they should encounter. Yet so unseasonable was the time, and so opposite was Captain Martin to anything, but only to fraught this ship also with his fantastical gold, as Captain Smith rather desired to relade her with cedar, which was a present dispatch, than either with dirt or the hopes and reports of an uncertain discovery, which he would perform when they had less charge and more leisure.

Whilst the conclusion was resolving, this happened. Powhatan, to express his love to Newport when he departed, presented him with twenty turkeys, conditionally to return him twenty swords, which immediately was sent him. Now after his departure he presented Captain Smith with the like luggage, but not finding his humor obeyed in not sending such weapons as he desired, he caused his people with twenty devices to obtain them. At last by ambushes at our very ports they would take them perforce, surprise us at work, or any way, which was so long permitted they became so insolent there was no rule. The command from England was so straight not to offend them as our authority-bearers (keeping their houses) would rather be anything than peace-breakers.

This charitable humor prevailed till well it chanced they meddled with Captain Smith, who without further deliberation gave them such an encounter as some he so hunted up and down the isle, some he so terrified with whipping, beating, and imprisonment, as for revenge they surprised two of our foraging disorderly soldiers, and having assembled their forces, boldly threatened at our ports to force Smith to redeliver seven savages, which for their villainies he detained prisoners, or we were all but dead men. But to try their furies he sallied out amongst them, and in less than an hour he so hampered their insolence they brought them his two men, desiring peace without any further composition for their prisoners. Those he examined, and caused them all believe, by several volleys of shot, one of their companions was shot to death, because they would not confess their intents and plotters of those villainies.

And thus they all agreed in one point: They were directed only by Powhatan to obtain him our weapons, to cut our own throats, with the manner where, how, and when, which we plainly found most true and apparent. Yet he sent his messengers, and his dearest daughter Pocahontas with presents to excuse him of the injuries done by some rash untoward captains his subjects, desiring their liberties for this time, with the assurance of his love forever. After Smith had given the prisoners what correction he thought fit, used them well a day or two after, and then delivered them Pocahontas, for whose sake only he feigned to have saved their lives, and gave them liberty.

The patient Council that nothing would move to war with the savages, would gladly have wrangled with Captain Smith for his cruelty. Yet none was slain to any man's knowledge, but it brought them in such fear and obedience, as his very name would sufficiently affright them. Where before, we had sometime peace and war twice in a day, and very seldom a week but we had some treacherous villainy or other.

The freight of this ship being concluded to be cedar, by the diligence of the Master and Captain Smith she was quickly reladed. Master Scrivener was neither idle nor slow to follow all things at the fort. The ship being ready to set sail, Captain Martin, being always very sickly and unserviceable and desirous to enjoy the credit of his supposed art of finding the golden mine, was most willingly admitted to return for England.

CHAPTER THREE

First Chesapeake Voyage

June 2 to July 21, 1608

BY THE SUMMER OF 1608, *having been in Virginia for more than a year, Smith was out of patience with Ratcliffe and eager to explore the Chesapeake Bay. He was to make two seven-week journeys that summer, returning with detailed maps and more information about the natives and area resources than had ever been collected.*

He handpicked his 14 crewmen based on their skills, strength, and willingness to work. Among them were a doctor, a carpenter, a blacksmith, a fisherman, a fishmonger (to discriminate among edible species), a tailor (to repair sails and shirts), a laborer, a soldier, and six "gentlemen." The soldier, able and loyal Anas Todkill, wrote much of the log for the two voyages that Smith would undertake that summer.

The vessel was a rib-framed, 40-foot barge of two to three tons capacity. Though open to weather, it had a canvas tarpaulin to provide some protection. The barge was propelled by Viking-style rowing and a square lugsail (and possibly a jib) that could be rapidly deployed. It was a makeshift expedition vessel at best, a small craft for 15 men on a seven-week voyage. But it was to be an adventure, a chance to make history, and, if it meant hard work, it was still a variation from the monotonous labor at the settlement.

Stores aboard the boat included barrels of water, bread, and dried meat, but not nearly enough to last the entire voyage. They expected to make a living from the land and water. Smith also brought along writing materials, a compass, and an instrument (possibly a pocket-size quadrant) to measure latitude. He intended to map the area carefully and make extensive notes.

On June 2 the barge—towed by a supply ship—headed down the James. That night at Cape Henry, the adventurers dropped their towline and waved to the England-bound supply ship as it headed out to sea. The barge sailed north across the mouth of the Chesapeake Bay, steering by stars and compass. For the first week or so, Smith and his crew would explore up the eastern shore, investigating waterways and interviewing the locals. On June 3, at present-day Fisherman's Island, they encountered a couple of natives fishing for kingfish with bone-headed spears.

The Indians were suspicious at first, seeing a strange-looking party of scruffy white men packed into a long boat. But they loosened up and directed the explorers to Accomac town (near today's town of Cape Charles), about 15 miles north. Here they were welcomed by the werowance Kiptopeke, who told them of a weird recent event. Two of the local children had died; their grieving parents, moved by a dream, decided to go visit the corpses, which appeared to be alive. Nearly everybody who went to see this miracle shortly afterwards died, possibly from exposure to germs.

The Englishmen were feted with speeches, feasting, and dancing. After spending the night, they pushed off and headed north, exploring the bays, inlets, and creeks along the way. The waterways were deemed good for canoes, but not for ships. Seeing islands several miles offshore (probably Watts and Tangier), Smith directed the helmsman to steer for them, but one of the Chesapeake's legendary summer squalls came up from the southwest and ambushed them. Violent but fortunately short, the storm forced them to retreat back to the eastern shore mainland, where they continued north.

Looking for drinking water on the Wighcocomoco River (today's Pocomoke), they finally found some "puddle water." After searching vainly for two more days, they gave up and went on without water—to their later regret. Smith went upriver as far as modern-day Pocomoke City, Maryland, where he placed one of his many brass crosses to claim the land for the English crown.

Upon descending the Pocomoke, the crew made their way across Pocomoke Sound and through shallow Cedar Straits to Tangier Sound. Late in the afternoon of June 6, the crew was blasted by an even worse squall than two days before. This one blew out the sail and mast, and ripped up big waves that nearly sank the boat. The storm pinned them down for two days, with very little cover except a few ridges of loblolly pine surrounded by salt marsh. During the ordeal of waiting and watching the skies—during which they named their retreat Limbo Island—the tailor repaired the sail with shirts, while the others fixed or replaced the mast.

When the skies began clearing, the crew headed back east and nosed up the broad Nanticoke River. Here, instead of rain, they were showered with arrows. The short-statured natives ran along the bank, yelling and shooting. In the morning, some Indians presented themselves on the beach with baskets and began to dance, as though in welcome. Suspicious, the English discharged a volley of muskets, sending the natives tumbling to the ground.

The volley may seem both a little unfair and unwise, but Smith was probably only trying to frighten the Indians, and things got out of control. In any event, seeing smoke on the west side of the river, the crew rowed over and found fires burning beside several wigwams. But, again, the people had fled. The crew left some copper, beads, bells, and looking glasses, and made their way out of the river.

The next morning, four Indians who had been fishing in the sound came by. Not knowing what had happened the day before, they bade the English to stay. The Indians went away and quickly returned with some 20 more people, followed shortly by hundreds. A frenzied trading session ensued.

So after a very poor initial reception, the Nanticoke turned out to be a generous people, offering valuable information and, as was the custom, a hostage as pledge of good intentions. The crew considered them "the best merchants of all other savages." Living on the eastern shore gave them easy access to the Atlantic, where they collected small sea shells much in demand as trade goods by other tribes to the north. The result was that the Nanticoke had the finest furs that Smith and the crew saw in their travels, furs that came from colder northern climates.

Despite the trading abilities of the Nanticoke people, Smith saw little potential for profit to the Virginia Company there. He did, however, perk up when they "much extolled a great nation called Massawomecks" who lived far to the north. Here was a clue to what Smith was looking for: furs and that fabled Northwest Passage to the Orient. As soon as he could politely do so, he bade the Nanticoke farewell.

On June 11, now about halfway up the 200-mile-long bay, they crossed to the western shore and anchored under (current) Calvert Cliffs for the night.

Moving ever northward toward the head of the bay, the crew covered some 100 miles over the next two days, taking advantage of favorable winds and tides. The first inlet they explored along this stretch was the Patapsco River, which Smith dubbed the Bolus—clay along the banks reminded him of bole, a kind of red or yellowish clay with supposed medicinal properties. Tying off, the crew then climbed several miles up the steeply rising wooded hillside. They were baffled that the place was devoid of Indians. In fact, the locals had been run off by the Massawomeck and Susquehannock from the north.

The trip up the Bolus was a turning point. They had been crammed together for nearly two weeks; their bread was moldly; and they had just rowed all day in the summer heat and humidity. Grumbling turned to loud complaints, then to pleading for a return to Jamestown. It was time for a pep talk. Smith's speech rallied the crew enough to get them upbay a dozen miles from the Patapsco. But then the wind and weather conspired

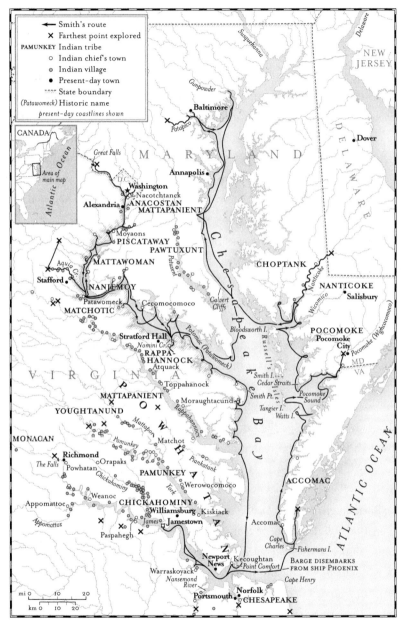

ROUTE OF SMITH'S FIRST CHESAPEAKE EXPEDITION,
JUNE 2 – JULY 21, 1608

against Smith. Furthermore, several men complained of illness from the bad bread. The captain relented. On June 15, he turned the barge back down the bay.

Within a day, they had sailed nearly one hundred miles south, and found themselves at the mouth of the Potomac River. Here, apparently buoyed in spirits, they began a long and adventurous digression. Smith had heard favorable rumors about the Potomac, and thus again stirred by the possibility of finding riches and a passage to the Orient, they headed upriver. For 30 miles they saw no inhabitants. Then they met two Indians who led them up Nomini Creek (on the Northern Neck, near today's Stratford, Virginia). Suddenly they were swarmed by Indians.

Hundreds of painted natives came pouring out of the woods, yelling like "spirits from hell." To frighten them, Smith ordered a volley of bullets that ricocheted off the water. Terrified, the Indians threw down their bows and arrows and agreed to exchange hostages.

The crew was on the trail of a possible big find. Newport had taken some bags of a "glistering metal" back to England, metal he had acquired—through trade—from Indians in the Potomac region. An assay proved it to contain silver. Visions of the good life urging them forward, Smith and his companions labored up the Potomac beyond the site of Washington, D.C. About six miles above the future capital, between today's Little Falls and Great Falls, they found waterfalls and rocky cliffs that in places showed a "spangled" deposit. They began digging in the sandy clay, but could not find anything they recognized as valuable.

Back downriver, the local werowance (the "King of Patawomeck") told them that what they were looking for was matchqueon, a silvery substance that warriors mixed with grease to smear on their faces and bodies. He sent them chasing up Aquia Creek, which empties into the west (Virginia) side of the Potomac near the present-day town of Stafford. They rowed the barge as far as they could, then got out and hiked about eight miles up through the woods to where the mine lay. The Indian guides were not happy about being chained together, until Smith, again showing himself a keen reader of human psychology, promised they could keep the chains when the hike was over.

The mine was a big hole that the Indians had dug in a hillside with shells and hatchets. After removing the ore, they washed it in a nearby crystal-clear brook, then put it in little bags to sell far and wide. Smith's guides loaded the scouting party with as much as they could carry. Back at the boat, Smith paid them for their trouble, then continued downriver. The mineral, it turns out, was probably antimony, a silvery-white crystalline mineral now used in alloys and semiconductors.

Though the area's mineral riches were doubtful, the crew did find an abundance of wildlife. There were so many fish, the crew tried to catch them with frying pans. For some reason the men had brought no nets.

Smith had spent an entire month exploring the Potomac; it was now July 15 and he still wanted to check out the Rappahannock, the next major river south, before returning home. Though their food supply was nearly spent and the crew eager to return, Smith could be very persuasive. He wanted to see the Indians he had met during his captivity, when Powhatan's warriors had paraded him from village to village. He had established friendly relations with many of them, and he remembered that the Rappahannock was large enough to merit careful exploration.

Rounding today's Smith Point, the crew emerged from the Potomac and hugged the crenellated Virginia shoreline as they steered downbay. They aimed for the south side of the Rappahannock's mouth but miscalculated the tide and ran the heavy barge aground on a shoal. While waiting for the tide to rise, the captain began amusing himself (and showing off) by spearing fish with his sword. Pretty soon everybody was doing it. Then Smith made a mistake. He speared a large flat fish and, not knowing what it was, reached out to take it off his sword. The fish, harmless looking enough, was a stingray with a barbed tail. The account of his accident shows how lucky he and his men were on their wilderness expedition.

With the captain's health still in doubt, they decided to save the Rappahannock for another trip and head home. Within a day they had made

CHESAPEAKE BARGE UNDER SAIL
(DETAIL OF SMITH'S 1612 MAP)

the 90 miles to the mouth of the James. Here they were welcomed by "simple savages" who, upon seeing the captain hurt, another crewman with a banged-up shin, and a boatload of bows, arrows, swords, shields, furs, and other booty, assumed that the expedition was returning in triumph from some great battle. Not to disappointment them, the crew entertained the natives with tales of whipping the dreaded Massawomeck. Sufficiently awed, the natives quickly spread the word.

Though it was a precarious perch on the edge of a vast untamed continent, Jamestown still felt like home to the voyagers, and as they approached they were exuberant enough to play a joke on the settlement. Before rounding the final bend, they trimmed the barge with painted streamers to make the boat look like a Spanish frigate. They had apparently carried such devices in case they spotted a Spanish vessel in the bay. Whether the settlers *fell for the ruse is unknown, but at least they refrained from firing upon the faux enemy and turning the homecoming into a tragedy.*

ON JULY 21 THE CREW DISEMBARKED at their humble fort. Things had changed in the seven weeks they had been away. A good portion of the colony was infirm. The others were fed up nearly to the point of mutiny against the ineffectual Ratcliffe. Instead of maintaining harmony, the president had been needlessly cruel, had hoarded the best food for himself, and had ordered the workers to construct a building in the woods for his own private use. The unreasonable order had stirred the ire of the colony, and a plot was afoot to take revenge.

The prodigality of the president's state went so deep into our small store that Smith and Scrivener tied him and his parasites to the rules of proportion. But now Smith being to depart, the president's authority so overswayed the discretion of Master Scrivener that our store, our time, our strength, and labors were idly consumed to fulfill his fantasies. The second of June 1608 Smith left the fort to perform his discovery with this company:

Walter Russell, *doctor of physic*

Gentlemen
Ralfe Murton.
Thomas Momford.
William Cantrill.
Richard Fetherstone.
James Burne.
Michael Sicklemore.

Soldiers
Jonas Profit, *fisher.*
Anas Todkill.

Robert Small.
James Watkins.
John Powell.

James Read, *blacksmith*.
Richard Keale, *fishmonger*.

These being in an open barge near three tons burthen, leaving the *Phoenix* at Cape Henry, they crossed the bay to the eastern shore, and fell with the isles called Smith's Isles, after our captain's name.

The first people we saw were two grim and stout savages upon Cape Charles, with long poles like javelins, headed with bone. They boldly demanded what we were and what we would. But after many circumstances they seemed very kind, and directed us to Accomac, the habitation of their werowance, where we were kindly entreated. This king was the comeliest, proper, civil savage we encountered. His country is a pleasant fertile clay soil, some small creeks, good harbors for small barks, but not for ships.

He told us of a strange accident lately happened him. And it was: Two children being dead, some extreme passions or dreaming visions, fantasies, or affection moved their parents again to revisit their dead carcasses, whose benumbed bodies reflected to the eyes of the beholders such delightful countenances, as though they had regained their vital spirits. This as a miracle drew many to behold them—all which being a great part of his people, not long after died, and but few escaped.

They spoke the language of Powhatan, wherein they made such descriptions of the bay, isles, and rivers that often did us exceeding pleasure.

Passing along the coast, searching every inlet and bay fit for harbors and habitations, seeing many isles in the midst of the bay, we bore up for them, but ere we could obtain them such an extreme gust of wind, rain, thunder, and lightning happened that with great danger we escaped the unmerciful raging of that ocean-like water. The highest land on the main, yet it was but low, we called Keale's Hill, and these uninhabited isles, Russell's Isles.

The next day, searching them for fresh water, we could find none; the defect whereof forced us to follow the next eastern channel, which brought us to the river of Wighcocomoco [*Pocomoke*]. The people at first with great fury seemed to assault us, yet at last with songs and dances and much mirth became very tractable. But searching their habitations for water, we could fill but three barricoes [*casks*], and that such puddle [*water*], that never till then we ever knew the want of good water. We dug and searched in many places, but before two days were expired we would have refused two barricoes of gold for one of that puddle water of Wighcocomoco.

Being past these isles which are many in number, but all naught for habitation, falling with a high land upon the main, we found a great pond of fresh water, but so exceeding hot we supposed it some bath. That place we called Point Ployer, in honor of that most honorable House of Moussaye in Brittany, that in an extreme extremity once relieved our captain. From Wighcocomoco to this place, all the coast is low broken Isles of Morap [*morass*], grown a mile or two in breadth and ten or twelve in length, good to cut for hay in summer and to catch fish and fowl in winter. But the land beyond them is all covered over with wood, as is the rest of the country.

Being thus refreshed in crossing over from the main to other isles, we discovered the wind and waters so much increased with thunder, lightning, and rain that our mast and sail blew overboard and such mighty waves over-racked us in that small barge that with great labor we kept her from sinking by freeing out the water.

Two days we were forced to inhabit these uninhabited isles, which for the extremity of gusts, thunder, rain, storms, and ill

INDIANS FISHING WITH SPEARS AND NETS
(THEODOR DE BRY, 1528-98)

weather we called Limbo. Repairing our sail with our shirts, we set sail for the main and fell with a pretty convenient river on the east called Kuskarawaok [Nanticoke].

The people ran as amazed in troops from place to place, and divers got into the tops of trees. They were not sparing of their arrows, nor the greatest passion they could express of their anger. Long they shot, we still riding at an anchor without their reach, making all the signs of friendship we could. The next day they came unarmed, with every one a basket, dancing in a ring, to draw us on shore. But seeing there was nothing in them but villainy, we discharged a volley of muskets charged with pistol shot; whereat they all lay tumbling on the ground, creeping some one way, some another into a great cluster of reeds hard by where their companies lay in ambush.

Toward the evening we weighed, and approaching the shore, discharging five or six shot among the reeds, we landed where there lay a many of baskets and much blood, but saw not a savage. A smoke appearing on the other side the river, we rowed thither, where we found two or three little houses, in each a fire. There we left some pieces of copper, beads, bells, and looking glasses, and then went into the bay. But when it was dark we came back again.

Early in the morning four savages came to us in their canoe, whom we used with such courtesy, not knowing what we were, nor had done, having been in the bay a-fishing. [They] bade us stay and ere long they would return, which they did and some twenty more with them; with whom after a little conference, two or three thousand men, women and children came clustering about us, every one presenting us with something, which a little bead would so well requite that we became such friends they would contend who should fetch us water, stay with us for hostage, conduct our men any whither, and give us the best content.

Here inhabit the people of Sarapinagh, Nause, Arseek, and Nanticoke, the best merchants of all other savages. They much extolled a great nation called Massawomecks, in search of whom we returned by Limbo. This river but only at the entrance is very narrow, and the people of small stature as them of Wighcocomoco—the land but low, yet it may prove very commodious, because it is but a ridge of land betwixt the bay and the main ocean.

Finding this eastern shore shallow broken isles, and for most part without fresh water, we passed by the straits of Limbo for the western shore. So broad is the bay here, we could scarce perceive the great high cliffs on the other side. By them we anchored that night and called them Rickard's Cliffs.

Thirty leagues we sailed more northwards, not finding any inhabitants, leaving all the eastern shore, low islands, but overgrown with wood, as all the coast beyond them so far as we could see. The western shore by which we sailed we found all along well watered but very mountainous and barren, the valleys very fertile but extremely thick of small wood so well as trees, and much frequented with wolves, bears, deer, and other wild beasts.

We passed many shallow creeks, but the first we found navigable for a ship, we called Bolus, for that the clay in many places under the cliffs by the high water mark did grow up in red and white knots as gum out of trees, and in some places so participated together as though they were all of one nature, excepting the color—the rest of the earth on both sides being hard sandy gravel, which made us think it bole armoniac and terra sigillata [*medicinal clays*].

When we first set sail, some of our gallants doubted nothing but that our captain would make too much haste home. But having lain in this small barge not above twelve or fourteen days, oft tired at the oars, our bread spoiled with wet so much that it was rotten (yet so good were their stomachs that they could digest it), they did with continual complaints so importune him now to return as caused him bespeak them in this manner:

"Gentlemen, if you would remember the memorable history of Sir Ralph Lane [*Roanoke Island colony commander, 1585-86*], how his company importuned him to proceed in the discovery of Moratico, alleging they had yet a dog that being boiled with sassafras leaves would richly feed them in their returns. Then what a shame would it be for you (that have been so suspicious of my tenderness) to force me return, with so much provision as we have, and scarce able to say where we have been, nor yet heard of that we were sent to seek.

"You cannot say but I have shared with you in the worst which is past. And for what is to come—of lodging, diet, or whatsoever—I am contented you allot the worst part to myself. As for your fears that I will lose myself in these unknown large waters, or be swallowed up in some stormy gust, abandon these childish fears, for worse than is past is not likely to happen, and there is as much danger to return as to proceed.

"Regain therefore your old spirits, for return I will not (if God please) till I have seen the Massawomecks, found Patawomeck, or the head of this water you conceit to be endless."

Two or three days we expected wind and weather, whose adverse of extremities added such discouragement that three or four fell sick, whose pitiful complaints caused us to return, leaving the bay some nine miles broad, at nine and ten fathoms water.

The 16 of June we fell with the river Patawomeck. Fear being gone and our men recovered, we were all content to take some pains to know the name of that seven-mile-broad river. For thirty miles sail, we could see no inhabitants. Then we were conducted by two savages up a little bayed creek, toward Onawmanient [near Nomini Bay], where all the woods were laid with ambushes to the number of three or four thousand savages [probably 300–400], so strangely painted, grimed, and disguised, shouting, yelling, and crying as so many spirits from hell could not have showed more terrible. Many bravados they made, but to appease their fury our captain prepared with as seeming a willingness as they to encounter them. But the grazing of our bullets upon the water (many being shot on purpose they might see them) with the echo of the woods so amazed them as down went their bows and arrows. And, exchanging hostages, James Watkins was sent six miles up the woods to their king's habitation.

We were kindly used of those savages, of whom we understood they were commanded to betray us by the direction of Powhatan. And he so directed from the discontents at Jamestown, because our captain did cause them stay in their country against their wills.

The like encounters we found at Patowomeck, Cecocawonee, and divers other places. But at Moyaones, Nacotchtant, and Toags the people did their best to content us.

Having gone so high as we could with the boat, we met divers savages in canoes, well loaden with the flesh of bears, deer, and other beasts, whereof we had part. Here we found mighty rocks growing in some places above the ground as high as the shrubby trees, and divers other solid quarries of divers tinctures. And divers places where the waters had fallen from the high mountains they had left a tinctured spangled scurf [deposit], that made many bare places seem as gilded. Digging the ground above in the highest cliffs of rocks, we saw it was a clay sand so mingled with yellow spangles as if it had been half pin-dust [dust from grinding brass pins].

In our return, inquiring still for this matchqueon [Indian word, possibly meaning "something pretty"], the king of Patawomeck gave us guides to conduct us up a little river called Quiyough [Aquia Creek], up which we rowed so high as we could. Leaving the boat with six shot and divers savages, he marched seven or eight mile before they came to the mine, leading his hostages in a small chain they were to have for their pains, being proud so richly to be adorned.

The mine is a great rocky mountain like antimony, wherein they dug a great hole with shells and hatchets. And hard by it runs a fair brook of crystal-like water, where they wash away the dross and keep the remainder, which they put in little bags and sell it all over the country to paint their bodies, faces, or idols, which makes them look like blackamoors dusted over with silver. With so much as we could carry we returned to our boat, kindly requiting this kind king and all his kind people.

The cause of this discovery [expedition] was to search this mine, of which Newport did assure us that those small bags (we had given him) in England he had tried to hold [prove] half silver. But all we got proved of no value.

Also [we came] to search what furs, the best whereof is at Kus-karawaok, where is made so much rawranoke (or white beads) that occasion as much dissension among the savages as gold and silver amongst Christians; and what other minerals, rivers, rocks, nations, woods, fishing, fruits, victual, and what other commodities the land afforded; and whether the bay were endless or how far it extended.

Of mines we were all ignorant. But a few beavers, otters, bears, martins and minks we found, and in divers places that abundance of fish, lying so thick with their heads above the water as for want of nets (our barge driving amongst them) we attempted to catch them with a frying pan. But we found it a bad instrument to catch fish with. Neither better fish, more plenty, nor more variety for small fish, had any of us ever seen in any place so swimming in the water. But they are not to be caught with frying pans!

Some small cod also we did see swim close by the shore by Smith's Isles, and some as high as Rickard's Cliffs. And some we have found dead upon the shore.

To express all our quarrels, treacheries, and encounters amongst those savages I should be too tedious. But in brief, at all times we so encountered them and curbed their insolence that they concluded with presents to purchase peace. Yet we lost not a man. At our first meeting our captain ever observed this order: to demand their bows and arrows, swords, mantles, and furs, with some child or two for hostage, whereby we could quickly perceive when they intended any villainy.

Having finished this discovery (though our victual was near spent), he intended to see his imprisonment acquaintances upon the river of Rappahannock (by many called Tappahannock). But our boat by reason of the ebb, chancing to ground upon a many shoals lying in the entrances, we spied many fishes lurking in the reeds. Our captain, sporting himself by nailing them to the ground with his sword, set us all a-fishing in that manner. Thus we took more in one hour than we could eat in a day.

But it chanced our captain, taking a fish from his sword (not knowing her condition), being much of the fashion of a thornback, but a long tail like a riding rod—whereon the midst is a most poisoned sting of two or three inches long—bearded like a saw on each side, which she struck into the wrist of his arm near an inch and a half. No blood nor wound was seen, but a little blue spot. But the torment was instantly so extreme that in four hours had so swollen his hand, arm, and shoulder we all with much sorrow concluded [*expected*] his funeral, and prepared his grave in an island by, as himself directed. Yet it pleased God by a precious oil Doctor Russell at the first applied to it when he sounded it with probe, ere night his tormenting pain was so well assuaged that he ate of the fish to his supper, which gave no less joy and content to us than ease to himself, for which we called the island Stingray Isle after the name of the fish.

Having neither surgeon nor surgery but that preservative oil we presently set sail for Jamestown, passing the mouths of the rivers of Piakatank and Pamunkey. The next day we safely arrived at Kecoughtan.

The simple savages seeing our captain hurt, and another bloody by breaking his shin, our numbers of bows, arrows, swords, mantles, and furs, would needs imagine we had been at wars. The truth of these accidents would not satisfy them, but impatiently importuned us to know with whom. Finding their aptness to believe, we failed not (as a great secret) to tell them anything that might affright them—what spoil we had got and made of the Massawomecks.

This rumor went faster up the river then our barge, that arrived at Warraskoyack the 20 of July, where trimming her with painted streamers and such devices as we could, we made them at Jamestown jealous of a Spanish frigate, where we all God be thanked safely arrived the 21 of July.

CHAPTER FOUR

Second Chesapeake Voyage

July 22 to September 9, 1608

THE RETURN OF SMITH *probably saved Ratcliffe, at least from punishment. Instead, he was merely deposed. Then, listening to the crew talk about their discoveries and the inflated but exciting news about the bay, the settlers clamored for Smith to take on the presidency. Smith was reluctant to do so for a couple of reasons. First of all, he was eager to embark on another Chesapeake voyage, to follow up on the places he had missed. Secondly, since Ratcliffe's one-year term was not due to expire for another two months, Smith was hesitant to step in. So the Council worked out an arrangement whereby the capable Matthew Scrivener, Council member since January, would serve as interim president until September, when a proper election would be held.*

Smith was indeed raring to go. Incredibly, within three days he was off again on a major voyage. During that long weekend the colony settled down, the barge was repaired and re-outfitted, and Smith's health returned enough for him to plan another seven-week expedition. This one would have a trimmed-down crew of twelve, plus the captain. Rejoining from the first expedition were nine toughened veterans. The only replacements were the tailor, the carpenter, a gentleman, and, interestingly, the physician. The log during the stingray incident makes a point of mentioning that they had no surgeon, only a medical doctor. This time they were taking along Anthony Bagnall, the surgeon who attended Smith on his return. Perhaps the Council agreed that the expedition would more likely need him than the colony.

On Sunday, July 24, 1608, the crew headed downriver again from Jamestown. The first expedition had journeyed nearly to the head of the bay and back, the men returning in reasonably good health. This trip would not be so lucky.

The goals of the second trip were more or less the same as the first: find precious metals and a short passage to the Orient. Also on the agenda was the remote possibility of finding the settlers from the Lost Colony, of whom there had been rumors but no conclusive proof. If the settlers were alive, they could furnish invaluable information about the land. Of these goals, Smith held out the most hope for finding a route to the Orient. Armchair geographers in Europe had for more than a century (since before the time of Columbus) convinced themselves that Asia was not far on the other side of North America. No one knew the true width of the continent, but they had the calculations to prove that it had a Panama-like isthmus somewhere in the north or else a series of navigable waterways leading out to the Pacific. While Smith was beginning to doubt this, it really did not matter—he was at heart an explorer, and whatever was out there, he wanted to discover it. The fact that there were still major places left unexplored in the Chesapeake nagged him. On this trip, then, he would focus on the head of the bay and on the Rappahannock.

By the second day, July 25, 1608, the barge was at the Indian village of Kecoughtan at the mouth of the James. With the wind blowing from the northeast—and the vessel unable to make much headway north under such conditions—the crew stayed on for a couple of days. Smith entertained the locals by firing off rockets. The display, of course, was not purely a spectacle; it reminded the Indians, and everyone in their far-reaching news network, that the English, though vastly outnumbered, had far superior weapons and thus greater power. Smith used the layover to let the Kecoughtan think he was going off to fight the hated Massawomeck.

On July 27 the wind shifted and Smith made haste to leave. The first day out in the bay, they sailed 45 miles, all the way up to Stingray Point at the lower lip of the Rappahannock. Leaving this river for their return trip, they continued north beyond the Potomac to the Patapsco River. On their previous trip they had reached about 12 miles beyond the Patapsco before weather and sickness forced them to turn back. Now, on around July 30, they sailed beyond their previous mark and into new territory, where illness threatened again.

The log reports that several men "were sick almost to death until they were seasoned to the country." Of the eight people (all from the last supply ship) who got sick, six of them had just been out on the previous trip, but were still not acclimated to the climate and whatever bacteria in the water and food their bodies had to adjust to. Only the people who had arrived over a year ago (with the first ships) did not get sick at this point. At any rate, somehow those unlucky eight were all heaving their guts out at the same time, too wasted to sit up, much less be of any use. And at this point, Smith suddenly needed every man he had.

Sailing to the head of the bay, the crew encountered Massawomecks in canoes. The dreaded Massawomeck lived up to their reputation by preparing immediately to assault the barge. With only five able-bodied men, the captain had to think fast. Instead of retreating, Smith decided to mount a charge. Improvising on a trick he had learned fighting the Turks several years back, he put hats on sticks along the barge's gunwales. The ruse worked.

The Massawomeck owned the only birchbark canoes on the Chesapeake. They were much faster and more maneuverable than the other tribes' dugouts, but were no match for the apparent magic of the white men's sail. Now with the upper hand (or perhaps realizing the Indians had meant no harm), Smith tried to entice them over to the barge. At first they would have none of it. Eventually two came paddling, unarmed. They may have heard of Europeans, but it is doubtful any of them had ever seen one, much less a sailing ship.

The captain invited the two braves aboard and presented them each with a little bell. They did not speak Powhatan, so the captain had to use sign language. The novelty of the bells and the friendly gesturing reassured them enough to invite the rest of their party onto the barge. A quick trading session followed. The Indians showed off their wounds, recently acquired in battle with the Tockwogh, their old enemies on the east side of the bay. The Massowomecks headed home for the night, apparently agreeing to meet the barge in the morning. But they never showed up.

Instead of waiting around, the crew decided to head right into the thick of the Massowomeck enemy's country. So they began moving up the Tockwogh (Sassafras) River. Instantly they were surrounded by a fleet of armed boats. After a few uneasy minutes, Smith discovered that one of the Tockwogh could speak Powhatan, and the others agreed to a friendly parley. The Tockwogh were particularly impressed by the Englishmen's recently acquired weapons, which bore Massowomeck insignia. Using the same stratagem he had with the Kecoughtan, Smith informed them that his crew had just defeated the Massowomeck and taken spoils. The story gave them instant status, and they were welcomed as heroes into a palisaded town, seven miles upriver.

During the traditional exchange of presents, Smith and others noticed that the Tockwogh had a lot of hatchets and knives and other iron and brass implements that would have been rare among the Powhatan tribes. Smith asked where it all had come from. The translator told him that it came from the Susquehannock, who—like just about everybody else around the bay—were mortal enemies of the Massawomeck. Naturally Smith wanted to meet these people and see what they knew about the region—any clue he could gather might pay off. Smith knew by then that the Susquehanna was the main branch at the head of the bay.

So the Tockwogh interpreter rounded up another interpreter, one who could speak Susquehannock. The idea was that one would translate from Susquehannock (an Iroquoian language) into Tockwogh, and the other would translate from Tockwogh into Powhatan. Then Smith, with his rudimentary Powhatan, would try to make sense of what was said. They headed downriver in the barge, crossed the bay, and anchored near the mouth of the Susquehanna. The interpreters got out and went on alone to see what they could arrange—perhaps they thought it better not to go en masse. Anyway, the barge could not make it beyond the falls, and the first Susquehannock village lay two days beyond (probably near modern-day Safe Harbor, Pennsylvania, more than 30 miles upriver).

Smith traveled upriver a few miles to what he named Smith's Falls. There he planted a cross to claim the river for England and to (unintentionally) puzzle any Indians who happened along. At other places the explorers put notes in trees or carved crosses into the bark. None of these crosses have ever been found.

Then, just about the time the translators were expected back, some 60 "giant-like" people came down the river. The translators must have made a good sell about the worth of these white allies, because the Susquehannocks were loaded with gifts—venison, wicker baskets, shields, bows, arrows, and three-foot-long pipes. A picture on Smith's map (dated 1612) shows a smiling, muscular chief wearing a fringed breechcloth, with a fox pelt over his shoulders. He holds a longbow in his right hand and a war club in his left. The hair on the right side of his head is shoulder-length, but the left side is shaven, according to the fashion of many Chesapeake Indians.

Five chiefs then came aboard and headed back across the bay. They watched in wonder as the crewmen recited their daily psalm. Then they began their own ritual, devised for this special occasion. They held their hands up to the sun and began singing. To Smith's chagrin they began adulating him as though he too were the sun. One can only imagine how otherworldly this must have sounded to European ears. Though Smith was a reluctant god, they decked him out with a great painted bearskin and a huge necklace of white beads. To top it all, they stroked his neck ceremoniously, promising food and aid if he would only stay and be their governor and defend and revenge them against the Massawomeck.

How could the Indians know that the English derived their power from a thin supply chain that stretched across the Atlantic? To them these 13 Englishmen seemed invincible, the Anglican religious rites further proof of their magic power. Smith said no, yet promised to return the following year. He never did. It is possible that he misunderstood and that they only wanted an alliance, not a new ruler.

The Susquehannock had heard of Powhatan but did not know much about him. One intriguing piece of information Smith obtained, though, was about people who lived "upon a great water beyond the mountains." At first the crew may have thought this at last was the way to the Pacific, but at some point they realized the Indians were talking about a lake or river in Canada, from which they had acquired French hatchets and other commodities. The French had only a month earlier begun settling Québec.

Convinced now that he had seen all the rivers and inlets worth note in the north, Smith decided to head back down the bay. On August 8 the crew sailed south. Smith wanted to get back to Jamestown in time for the September 10 elections, but there was still time for one more major exploratory probe. He had now explored all three of the Chesapeake's largest rivers—the Susquehanna, the Potomac, and the James. But the Rappahannock was also big, and still unmapped—it was worth a try. Instead of the usual barrier of rocks and falls, it might have the secret passage he sought. Unfortunately, after two weeks of friendly interaction with Indians, things were about to change.

On August 14, 1608, the barge sailed past the Potomac, rounded the Northern Neck, and proceeded up the Rappahannock. After about 30 miles, they stopped at the village of Moraughtacund, where they were greeted by their "old friend Mosco." Apparently they had met him on the Potomac on their earlier trip. From his appearance, Smith thought him of French extraction, though he was more likely Spanish—the Spanish had briefly visited the bay 20 years back. He welcomed the similarly bearded English as brothers and made himself extremely useful as a laborer and guide.

Mosco warned them that since they had made friends with the Moraughtacund they should not travel to the Rappahannock, who lived several more miles upstream. It seems the Moraughtacund had recently kidnapped three wives of the Rappahannock chief, and he was not happy about it. Smith interpreted this story as simply a way for the Moraughtacund to keep the English trade to themselves. He should have trusted Mosco.

Upriver, a dozen or so Rappahannock beckoned the barge to a little creek. Waiting there were some canoes loaded with trade goods. As a precaution, Smith demanded a good-faith exchange of hostages, "in sign of love" as the quaint expression went. After talking it over, a few unarmed Indians came forward with their man. The stalwart Anas Todkill was selected (or volunteered) to serve as the English hostage, but first he wanted to have a look around. Though the Indians objected, he somehow managed to get a couple of hundred yards up into the clearing and saw, positioned behind the trees, a small battalion of Indians waiting, he believed, in ambush. When he tried to return to the boat, he was grabbed. He yelled out that they were betrayed.

A small battle began, the English relying on the nearly impenetrable shields of the Massowomeck to mount a rescue of Todkill. They then took the Rappahannock's canoes and presented them to Mosco, along with some arrows. But they broke most of the arrows they found—a major loss to the Rappahannock, since it took a man a full day to make a single arrow. The crew had learned its lesson. Returning to Moraughtacund, they spent the rest of the day armoring the barge with Massawomeck shields.

Not to be deterred, they started back up the river the very next morning. With the Rappahannock villages located along the northern shore, the barge kept to the opposite side. About 25 miles upriver, near some high white clay cliffs, about 30 to 40 Indians waited, camouflaged as bushes growing amid the sedge. When the barge was within range, arrows began whistling through the air. They hit the shields and fell harmlessly into the river. Smith answered with a volley of musket shot, but it must not have done much damage, for a little later the Indians were on the shore, dancing and singing "very merrily"—no doubt in derision.

Farther upriver the English had a much better reception, being entertained at three villages. But just beyond, the crew suffered a sad loss. Richard Fetherstone, veteran of the first voyage, died—possibly of malaria or heatstroke.

The next day they made the river's fall line (today's Fredericksburg), where they went ashore and planted a brass cross. While others were out looking for fresh water and valuable minerals and herbs, the sentinel at the barge saw an arrow land nearby. He sounded the alarm, and the advance group raced back to the boat. Suddenly there were arrows everywhere. Taking cover behind trees, the English returned fire, but Smith credited Mosco for saving the day.

Shooting arrows and dashing back and forth from the barge like a madman, he gave the impression that "there were many savages" on the English side. As the enemy departed, he even ran after them until they were out of sight. One Indian, wounded in the knee, had been left behind. Mosco was in favor of beating his brains out on the spot. Taking a more lenient approach, Smith had Bagnall treat his wounds; afterwards he took some food and answered Smith's questions. His complicated tale reveals the complexity of tribal relationships in the area.

Waiting until dark, the crew began quietly slipping down the river, which was uncomfortably narrow at this point. Mannahoack Indians attacked almost immediately. Arrows hit the barge and its shields, but the crew remained miraculously unharmed. Amoroleck, the captive, tried to yell to his countrymen that he was okay, but over the din of battle he could not make himself heard. Surging downriver about 12 miles by dawn, Smith finally decided to anchor in a broad bay, out of arrow range.

The Mannahoack appeared on the shore. Convinced that it was futile to try to harm these Englishmen, the warriors hung their bows in trees and laid down their arrows. Afterwards the four kings met with Smith and crew on shore to talk and trade. The peace well established, the crew left some 500 Indians "singing, dancing, and making merry."

Back in Rappahannock territory, the Indians rejoiced that the English had beaten the Mannahoack, their enemies. Like other tribes, they were convinced that the spoils of war (in this case, Mannahoack bows and arrows) meant a victory, not a peace. Seeming to forget that they themselves had recently tried to destroy the Englishmen, they suddenly wanted to be friends. Smith now had leverage, and he used it. He told them that they had twice assaulted him, and now he was ready to destroy their homes if they did not comply with his demands. Playing the part of a chief himself, Smith demanded that the Rappahannock present him the king's bows and arrows, and not dare to come into his presence armed. In addition, he wanted them to make peace with the Moraughtacund, who were his friends. Finally, he wanted the Rappahannock king's son as a pledge.

To sort everything out, Smith proposed a meeting of chiefs at the place where they had first fought. At the meeting the Rappahannock chief agreed to every demand except the last—he could not bear to give up his only son. He offered instead to give Smith the three wives the Moraughtacund had stolen, thus starting the brouhaha in the first place. Smith thought it a fair deal. The only thing was, Smith (who never married) did not really want any Indian wives. So he divvied them up. Rappahannock got the first pick, the Moraughtacund chief the second, and the third he gave to Mosco.

Warring tribes at last embraced in friendship (no matter how temporary). They spent the rest of the day killing deer and preparing for the biggest bacchanalia they had had in a long time. The next day the feasting began. More than 600 Indians gathered and began dancing and singing. Mosco was so moved by the occasion that he changed his name to Uttasantasough to honor the English. Everybody promised the Englishmen to be their friends forever and plant corn for them.

Knowing such a celebration could go on for days, Smith and his crew, when they could gracefully take their leave, loaded into the barge and, with a salute of gunfire, disappeared downstream amid a tumult of shouts and well wishes. By the end of the day, August 31, the barge had made it back to the bay and was anchored in the Piankatank, the next river south.

After a quick trip up the Piankatank, the crew was almost finished with the second expedition. During a harrowing nighttime thunderstorm, Smith found Point Comfort only by flashes of lightning and rounded into the James on September 4, 1608. He then decided they had time for one last sidetrip.

They headed up a narrow river (possibly the Elizabeth), near the mouth of the James. The river becoming too narrow, and no Indians to be seen, they turned back and went up the adjacent Nansemond River. Here they saw a party of Indians tending their fishing weirs. The Indians immediately took off, but Smith sent a handful of men ashore with "toys." After finding the trinkets, some Indians began singing and dancing, inviting the barge to return.

Where the river constricted, Smith invited a few Indians aboard (probably as a precaution against attack), but they first wanted to go get their bows and arrows. When they came back and still refused to get on board, Smith suspected a trap. Sure enough, just upriver, two hundred or more archers, hidden along the banks, unleashed a barrage of arrows. (Of course, we have only Smith's word that it was the Indians who shot first.) Bagnall got shot in the hat and sleeve; otherwise the onslaught was remarkably ineffective. The trailing canoes joined in the melee, but the English quickly dispersed them with a few rounds.

The crew then pulled in the empty dugouts and began chopping them up. They did this work in plain view, knowing that it was tantamount to destroying the Indians' livelihood—it could take weeks to replace their fleet, a painstaking process of hollowing out tree trunks with fire and sharp stones and shells. The Indians right away lay down their bows and signified they wanted to make peace. As with the Rappahannock, Smith demanded they bring him the chief's bows and arrows, as a sign of submission. He also demanded a chain of pearls and 400 baskets of corn. If they did not comply *he would destroy all the canoes, burn their corn and their houses, and lay waste everything they owned.*

They requested a canoe to undertake this business, and the crew imperiously shoved one out into the river. Smith told them to swim for it. The Indians then busily went about complying with his orders, fetching basket after basket of corn. Smith presumably then gave them back their other canoes. The Englishmen, their dominance established, bid the Indians farewell and sailed for home. After more than a thousand miles, the explorers arrived back in Jamestown on September 7.

THERE [*IN JAMESTOWN*] WE FOUND the last supply were all sick, the rest—some lame, some bruised, all unable to do anything but complain of the pride and unreasonable needless cruelty of the silly president that had riotously consumed the store. And to fulfill his follies about building him an unnecessary building for his pleasure in the woods, [he] had brought them all to that misery that had we not arrived they had as strangely tormented him with revenge. But the good news of our discovery, and the good hope we had by the savages' relation that our bay had stretched into the South Sea (or somewhat near it), appeased their fury.

But conditionally [*the colonists urged*] that Ratcliffe should be deposed, and that Captain Smith would take upon him the government, as by course it did belong. Their request being effected, he substituted Master Scrivener his dear friend in the presidency, equally distributing those private provisions the other had engrossed, appointing more honest officers to assist Master Scrivener (who then lay exceeding sick of a fever). And in regard of the weakness of the company and heat of the year, they being unable to work, he left them to live at ease, to recover their healths, but embarked himself to finish his discovery.

The 24 of July, Captain Smith set forward to finish the discovery with twelve men. Their names were:

Gentlemen
Nathaniel Powell.
Thomas Momford.
Richard Fetherstone.
Michael Sicklemore.
James Bourne.
Anthony Bagnall, *Surgeon.*

Soldiers.
Jonas Profit.
Anas Todkill.
Edward Pising.
Richard Keale.
James Watkins.
William Ward.

The wind being contrary caused our stay two or three days at Kecoughtan. The king feasted us with much mirth; his people were persuaded we went purposely to be revenged of the Massawomecks.

In the evening we fired a few rockets, which flying in the air so terrified the poor savages they supposed nothing unpossible we attempted, and desired to assist us.

The first night we anchored at Stingray Isle. The next day crossed Patawomeck's River, and hasted to the River Bolus. We went not much further before we might see the bay to divide in two heads, and arriving there we found it divided in four, all which we searched so far as we could sail them. Two of them we found inhabited, but in crossing the bay, we encountered seven or eight canoes full of Massawomecks. We, seeing them prepare to assault us, left our oars and made way with our sail to encounter them. Yet were we but five with our captain that could stand, for within two days after we left Kecoughtan, the rest (being all of the last supply) were sick almost to death until they were seasoned to the country.

Having shut them under our tarpaulin, we put their hats upon sticks by the barge's side, and betwixt two hats a man with two pieces, to make us seem many. And so we think the Indians supposed those hats to be men, for they fled with all possible speed to the shore, and there stayed, staring at the sailing of our barge till we anchored right against them.

Long it was ere we could draw them to come unto us. At last they sent two of their company unarmed in a canoe; the rest all followed to second them if need required. These two being but each presented with a bell, brought aboard all their fellows, presenting our captain with venison, bear's flesh, fish, bows, arrows, clubs, targets, and bearskins. We understood them nothing at all but by signs, whereby they signified unto us they had been at wars with the Tockwoghs, the which they confirmed by showing us their green [*fresh*] wounds. But the night parting us, we imagined they appointed the next morning to meet, but after that we never saw them.

Entering the river of Tockwogh, the savages all armed, in a fleet of boats, after their barbarous manner, round environed us. So it chanced one of them could speak the language of Powhatan, who persuaded the rest to a friendly parley. But when they saw us furnished with the Massawomecks' weapons, and we, feigning the invention of Kecoughtan, to have taken them perforce, they conducted us to their palisaded town, mantled with the barks of trees, with scaffolds like mounts, breasted about with breasts very formally. Their men, women, and children with dances, songs, fruits, furs, and what they had, kindly welcomed us, spreading mats for us to sit on, stretching their best abilities to express their loves.

Many hatchets, knives, pieces of iron, and brass, we saw amongst them, which they reported to have from the Susquehannocks, a mighty people and mortal enemies with the Massawomecks.

The Sasques-ahanougs are a Gyant like peo=ple & thus a-tyred

epewig

Vtchowig

S A S Q V E

Tesingh

Attaock   S H A N

Qnadroque

SUSQUEHANNOCK CHIEF WITH BOW AND WAR CLUB
(INSET FROM SMITH'S 1612 MAP)

The Susquehannocks inhabit upon the chief spring of these four branches of the bay's head, two days' journey higher than our barge could pass for rocks. Yet we prevailed with the interpreter to take with him another interpreter, to persuade the Susquehannocks to come visit us, for their languages are different. Three or four days we expected their return.

Then sixty of those giant-like people came down, with presents of venison, tobacco pipes three foot in length, baskets, targets, bows, and arrows. Five of their chief werowances came boldly aboard us to cross the bay for Tockwogh, leaving their men and canoes; the wind being so high they durst not pass.

Our order was daily to have prayer with a psalm, at which solemnity the poor savages much wondered. Our prayers being done, a while they were busied with a consultation till they had contrived their business. Then they began in a most passionate manner to hold up their hands to the sun, with a most fearful song. Then embracing our captain, they began to adore him in like manner. Though he rebuked them, yet they proceeded till their song was finished; which done, with a most strange furious action and a hellish voice, began an oration of their loves. That ended, with a great painted bearskin they covered him. Then one ready with a great chain of white beads, weighing at least six or seven pounds, hung it about his neck. The others had 18 mantles, made of divers sorts of skins sewed together. All these with many other toys they laid at his feet, stroking their ceremonious hands about his neck for his creation to be their governor and protector, promising their aids, victuals, or what they had to be his if he would stay with them, to defend and revenge them of the Massawomecks.

But we left them at Tockwogh, sorrowing for our departure. Yet we promised the next year again to visit them.

Many descriptions and discourses they made us, of Atquana-chuke, Massawomeck, and other people, signifying they inhabit

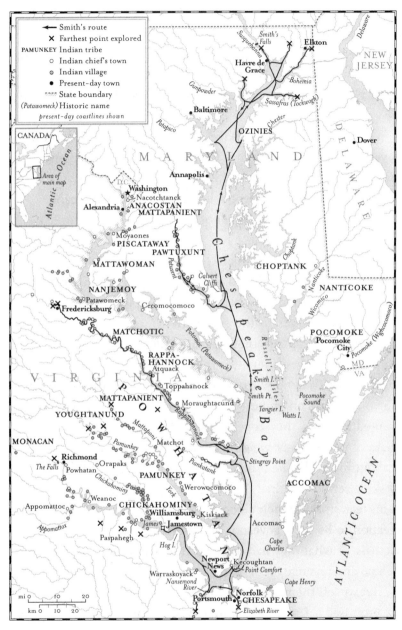

ROUTE OF SMITH'S SECOND CHESAPEAKE EXPEDITION,
JULY 29 – SEPTEMBER 7, 1608

upon a great water beyond the mountains, which we understood to be some great lake or the river of Canada, and from the French to have their hatchets and commodities by trade. These know no more of the territories of Powhatan than his name, and he as little of them but [that] the Atquanachukes are on the ocean sea.

The highest mountain we saw northward we called Peregrine's Mount, and a rocky river, where the Massawomecks went up, Willowbyes River, in honor of the town our captain was born in and that honorable house the Lord Willoughby, his most honored good friend. The Susquehannocks' river we called Smith's Falls; the next point to Tockwogh, Pising's Point; the next it Point Bourne. Powell's Isles and Smal's Point is by the River Bolus, and the little bay at the head Profit's Pool. Watkins', Read's, and Momford's Points are on each side Limbo; Ward, Cantrell, and Sicklemore betwixt Patawomeck and Pamunkey, after the names of the discoverers. In all those places and the farthest we came up the rivers, we cut in trees so many crosses as we would, and in many places made holes in trees wherein we wrote notes, and in some places crosses of brass, to signify to any: Englishmen had been there.

Thus having sought all the inlets and rivers worth noting, we returned to discover the river of Pawtuxunt. These people we found very tractable, and more civil than any. We promised them, as also the Patawomecks, to revenge them of the Massawomecks, but our purposes were crossed.

In the discovery of this river some call Rappahannock, we were kindly entertained by the people of Moraughtacund. Here we encountered our old friend Mosco, a lusty savage of Wighcocomoco [different from the village of the same name across the bay] upon the river of Patawomeck. We supposed him some Frenchman's son, because he had a thick black bushy beard (and the savages seldom have any at all), of which he was not a little proud to see so many of his countrymen. Wood and water he would fetch us, guide us any whither, nay, cause divers of his countrymen help us tow against wind or tide from place to place till we came to Patawomeck. There he rested till we returned from the head of the river, and occasioned our conduct to the mine we supposed antimony.

And in the place [*Moraughtacund*] he failed not to do us all the good he could, persuading us in any case not to go to the Rappahannocks, for they would kill us for being friends with the Moraughtacunds that but lately had stolen three of the king's women. This we did think was but that his friends might only have our trade, so we crossed the river to the Rappahannocks.

There some twelve or sixteen standing on the shore directed us a little creek where was good landing, and commodities for us in three or four canoes we saw lie there. But according to our custom, we demanded to exchange a man in sign of love, which after they had a little consulted, four or five came up to the middles to fetch our man and leave us one of them, showing we need not fear them, for they had neither clubs, bows, nor arrows.

Notwithstanding, Anas Todkill, being sent on shore to see if he could discover any ambushes, or what they had, desired to go over the plain to fetch some wood. But they were unwilling, except we would come into the creek, where the boat might come close ashore. Todkill by degrees, having got some two stones' throws up the plain, perceived two or three hundred men (as he thought) behind the trees, so that offering [*attempting*] to return to the boat, the savages assayed to carry him away perforce, that he called to us we were betrayed. And by that he had spoke the word, our hostage was overboard. But Watkins his keeper slew him in the water.

Immediately we let fly amongst them, so that they fled, and Todkill escaped. Yet they shot so fast that he fell flat on the ground ere he could recover the boat. Here the Massawomeck targets stood us in good stead, for upon Mosco's words we had set them about the forepart of our boat like a forecastle, from whence we securely beat

WARRIOR WITH SIGNATURE MARKINGS ON HIS BACK
(THEODOR DE BRY, 1528-98)

the savages from off the plain without any hurt. Yet they shot more than a thousand arrows, and then fled into the woods.

Arming ourselves with these light targets (which are made of little small sticks woven betwixt strings of their hemp and silk grass, as is our cloth, but so firmly that no arrow can possibly pierce them), we rescued Todkill, who was all bloody by some of them who were shot by us that held him. But as God pleased he had no hurt; and following them up to the woods, we found some slain, and in divers places much blood. It seems all their arrows were spent, for we heard no more of them. Their canoes we took; the arrows we found we broke, save them we kept for Mosco, to whom we gave the canoes for his kindness that entertained us in the best triumphing manner and warlike order in arms of conquest he could procure of the Moraughtacunds.

The rest of the day we spent in accommodating our boat. Instead of tholes [*oarlock pegs*] we made sticks like bedstaves,

INDIAN HUNTERS DISGUISED IN DEERSKINS
(FRENCH SOLDIER, 1600s)

to which we fastened so many of our Massawomeck targets that environed her as waistcloths.

The next morning we went up the river, and our friend Mosco followed us along the shore and at last desired to go with us in our boat. But as we passed by Pissaseck, Matchopeak, and Mecuppom—three towns situated upon high white clay cliffs, the other side all a low plain marsh and the river there but narrow—thirty or forty of the Rappahannocks had so accommodated themselves with branches as we took them for little bushes growing among the sedge. Still, seeing their arrows strike the targets and dropped in the river, whereat Mosco fell flat in the boat on his face, crying, "the Rappahannocks!"— which presently we espied to be the bushes, which at our first volley fell down in the sedge. When we were near half a mile from them, they showed themselves dancing and singing very merrily.

The kings of Pissaseck, Nantaughtacund, and Cuttatawomen used us kindly, and all their people neglected not anything to Mosco to bring us to them.

Betwixt Secobeck and Massawteck is a small isle or two, which causes the river to be broader than ordinary. There it pleased God to take one of our company called Master Fetherstone, that all the time he had been in this country had behaved himself honestly, valiantly, and industriously. Where in a little bay we called Fetherstone's Bay, we buried him with a volley of shot. The rest notwithstanding their ill diet and bad lodging—crowded in so small a barge, in so many dangers never resting, but always tossed to and again—had all well recovered their healths.

The next day we sailed so high as our boat would float [*falls at Fredericksburg, Virginia*], there setting up crosses and engraving our names in the trees. Our sentinel saw an arrow fall by him, though we had ranged up and down more than an hour in digging in the earth, looking of stones, herbs, and springs, not seeing where a savage could well hide himself.

Upon the alarum by that we had recovered our arms. There was about a hundred nimble Indians skipping from tree to tree, letting fly their arrows so fast as they could. The trees here served us for barricades as well as they. But Mosco did us more service than we expected, for having shot away his quiver of arrows, he ran to the boat for more. The arrows of Mosco at the first made them pause upon the matter, thinking by his bruit and skipping there were many savages. About half an hour this continued; then they all vanished as suddenly as they approached. Mosco followed them so far as he could see us, till they were out of sight.

As we returned there lay a savage as dead, shot in the knee, but taking him up we found he had life, which Mosco seeing, never was dog more furious against a bear than Mosco was to have beat out his brains. So we had him to our boat, where our surgeon, who went with us to cure our captain's hurt of the stingray, so dressed this savage that within an hour after, he looked somewhat cheerfully, and did eat and speak.

In the meantime we contented Mosco in helping him to gather up their arrows, which were an armful, whereof he gloried not a little. Then we desired Mosco to know what he [the prisoner] was, and what countries were beyond the mountains. The poor savage mildly answered: He and all with him were of Hassinunga, where there are three kings more like unto them—namely, the king of Stegara, the king of Tanxnitania, and the king of Shackakonea, that were come to Mahaskahod, which is only a hunting town, and the bounds betwixt the kingdom of the Mannahoacks and the Nantaughtacunds, but hard by where we were. We demanded why they came in that manner to betray us that came to them in peace and to seek their loves. He answered: They heard we were a people come from under the world, to take their world from them. We asked him how many worlds he did know; he replied, he knew no more but that which was under the sky that covered him, which were the Powhatans, with the Monacans, and the Massawomecks that were higher up in the mountains. Then we asked him what was beyond the mountains. He answered the sun, but of anything else he knew nothing because the woods were not burnt. They cannot travel but where the woods are burnt.

These and many such questions we demanded, concerning the Massawomecks, the Monacans, their own country, and where were the kings of Stegara, Tanxnitania, and the rest. The Monacans, he said, were their neighbors and friends, and did dwell as they in the hilly countries by small rivers, living upon roots and fruits, but chiefly by hunting. The Massawomecks did dwell upon a great water, and had many boats and so many men that they made war with all the world. For their kings, they were gone every one a several way with their men on hunting. But those with him came thither a-fishing till they saw us. Notwithstanding, they would be altogether at night at Mahaskahod.

For his relation we gave him many toys, with persuasions to go with us, and he as earnestly desired us to stay [await] the coming of those kings that for his good usage should be friends with us, for he was brother to Hassinunga. But Mosco advised us presently to be gone, for they were all naught. Yet we told him we would not till it was night. All things we made ready to entertain what came, and Mosco was as diligent in trimming his arrows.

The night being come, we all embarked, for the river was so narrow had it been light the land on the one side was so high they might have done us exceeding much mischief. All this while the King of Hassinunga was seeking the rest, and had consultation a good time what to do. But by their spies seeing we were gone, it was not long before we heard their arrows dropping on every side the boat. We caused our savages to call unto them, but such a yelling and hallowing they made that they heard nothing, but now and then a piece, aiming so near as we could where we heard the most voices.

More than twelve miles they followed us in this manner. Then, the day appearing, we found ourselves in a broad bay, out of danger of their shot, where we came to an anchor and fell to breakfast. Not so much as speaking to them till the sun was risen, being well refreshed, we untied our targets that covered us as a deck and all showed ourselves with those shields on our arms and swords in our hands, and also our prisoner Amoroleck. A long discourse there was betwixt his countrymen and him—how good we were, how well we used him, how we had a Patawomeck with us [who] loved us as his life that would have slain him had we not preserved him, and that he should have his liberty would they be but friends; and to do us any hurt it was impossible.

Upon this they all hung their bows and quivers upon the trees, and one came swimming aboard us with a bow tied on his head, and another with a quiver of arrows, which they delivered our captain as a present. The captain having used them so kindly as he could, told them the other three kings should do the like, and then the great king of our world should be their friend, whose men we were. It was no sooner demanded but performed.

So upon a low moorish [*boggy*] point of land we went to the shore where those four kings came and received Amoroleck. Nothing they had but bows, arrows, tobacco bags, and pipes. What we desired, none refused to give us, wondering at everything we had, and heard we had done. Our pistols they took for pipes, which they much desired, but we did content them with other commodities. And so we left four or five hundred of our merry Mannahoacks, singing, dancing, and making merry, and set sail for Moraughtacund.

In our returns we visited all our friends, [*who*] rejoiced much at our victory against the Mannahoacks, who many times had wars also with them. But now they were friends and desired we would be friends with the Rappahannocks, as we were with the Mannahoacks. Our captain told them they had twice assaulted him that came only in love to do them good, and therefore he would now burn all their houses, destroy their corn, and forever hold them his enemies, till they made him satisfaction. They desired to know what that should be. He told them they should present him the king's bow and arrows, and not offer to come armed where he was, that they should be friends with the Moraughtacunds his friends, and give him their king's son in pledge to perform it. And then all King James his men should be their friends.

Upon this they presently sent to the Rappahannocks to meet him at the place where they first fought, where would be the kings of Nantaughtacund and Pissaseck, which according to their promise were there so soon as we, where Rappahannock presented his bow and arrows and confirmed all we desired, except his son. Having no more but him he could not live without him, but instead of his son he would give him the three women Moraughtacund had stolen. This was accepted, and so in three or four canoes so many as could went with us to Moraughtacund, where Mosco made them such relations, and gave to his friends so many bows and arrows, that they no less loved him than admired us.

The three women were brought our captain, to each he gave a chain of beads, and then, causing Moraughtacund, Mosco, and Rappahannock stand before him, bid Rappahannock take her he loved best, and Moraughtacund choose next, and to Mosco he gave the third. Upon this away went their canoes over the water to fetch their venison and all the provision they could, and they that wanted boats swam over the river. The dark commanded us then to rest.

The next day there was of men, women, and children, as we conjectured, six or seven hundred—dancing and singing, and not a bow nor arrow seen amongst them. Mosco changed his name [to] Uttasantasough, which we interpret "Stranger," for so they call us. All promising ever to be our friends, and to plant corn purposely for us, and we to provide hatchets, beads, and copper for them, we departed, giving them a volley of shot, and they us as loud shouts and cries as their strengths could utter.

That night we anchored in the river of Piankatank, and discovered [explored] it so high as it was navigable. But the people were most a-hunting, save a few old men, women, and children that were tending their corn, of which they promised us part when we would fetch it, as had done all the nations wherever we had yet been.

In a fair calm, rowing toward Point Comfort, we anchored in Gosnold's Bay, but such a sudden gust surprised us in the night with thunder and rain that we never thought more to have seen Jamestown. Yet running before the wind, we sometimes saw the land by the flashes of fire from heaven, by which light only we kept from the splitting shore, until it pleased God in that black darkness to preserve us by that light to find Point Comfort.

There refreshing ourselves, because we had only but heard of the Chesapeakes and Nansemonds, we thought it as fit to know all our neighbors near home as so many nations abroad.

So setting sail for the southern shore, we sailed up a narrow river up the country of Chesapeake. It hath a good channel, but many shoals about the entrance. By that we had sailed six or seven miles, we saw two or three little garden plots with their houses, the shores overgrown with the greatest pine and fir trees we ever saw in the country. But not seeing nor hearing any people, and the river very narrow, we returned to the great river to see if we could find any of them.

Coasting the shore toward Nansemond, which is most oyster banks, at the mouth of that river we spied six or seven savages making their weirs, who presently fled. Ashore we went, and where they wrought [reached] we threw divers toys, and so departed.

Far we were not gone ere they came again, and began to sing and dance and recall us. And thus we began our first acquaintance. At last, one of them desired us to go to his house up that river. Into our boat voluntarily he came; the rest ran after us by the shore with all show of love that could be.

Seven or eight miles we sailed up this narrow river. At last on the western shore we saw large cornfields, in the midst a little isle [probably Dumpling Island, Nansemond River, where a small Indian site has been uncovered], and in it was abundance of corn. The people he told us were all a-hunting, but in the isle was his house, to which he invited us with much kindness. To him, his wife, and children, we gave such things as they seemed much contented them.

The others being come, desired us also to go but a little higher to see their houses. Here our host left us; the rest rowed by us in a canoe, till we were so far past the isle the river became very narrow. Here we desired some of them to come aboard us, whereat pausing a little, they told us they would but fetch their bows and arrows and go all with us. But being ashore and thus armed, they persuaded us to go forward, but we could neither persuade them into their canoe, nor into our boat. This gave us cause to provide for the worst.

MAKING A CANOE WITH FIRE AND SHELL SCRAPERS
(THEODOR DE BRY, 1528-98)

Far we went not ere seven or eight canoes full of men armed appeared following us, staying to see the conclusion. Presently from each side the river came arrows so fast as two or three hundred could shoot them, whereat we returned to get the open [water]. They in the canoes let fly also as fast. But amongst them we bestowed so many shot the most of them leaped overboard and swam ashore, but two or three escaped by rowing. Being against their plains [meadows], our muskets they found shot farther than their bows, for we made not twenty shot ere they all retired behind the next trees.

Being thus got out of their trap, we seized on all their canoes and moored them in the midst of the open. More than a hundred arrows stuck in our targets and about the boat, yet none hurt. Only Anthony Bagnall was shot in his hat, and another in his sleeve. But seeing their multitudes, and suspecting as it was that both the

Nansemonds and the Chesapeakes were together, we thought it best to ride by their canoes awhile, to bethink if it were better to burn all in the isle, or draw them to composition [*cease-fire*], till we were provided to take all they had, which was sufficient to feed all our colony. But to burn the isle at night it was concluded.

In the interim we began to cut in pieces their canoes, and they presently to lay down their bows, making signs of peace. Peace we told them we would accept, would they bring us their king's bows and arrows, with a chain of pearl, and when we came again give us four hundred baskets full of corn. Otherwise, we would break all their boats, and burn their houses and corn and all they had. To perform all this they alleged only the want of a canoe; so we put one adrift and bade them swim to fetch her. And till they performed their promise, we would but only break their canoes. They cried to us to do no more—all should be as we would, which presently they performed. Away went their bows and arrows, and tag and rag came with their baskets. So much as we could carry we took, and so departing good friends, we returned to Jamestown, where we safely arrived the 7 of September 1608.

There we found Master Scrivener and divers others well recovered, many dead, some sick, the late president [*Ratcliffe*] prisoner for mutiny, by the honest diligence of Master Scrivener the harvest gathered, but the provision in the store much spoiled with rain.

Thus was that summer (when little wanted) consumed and spent, and nothing done, such was the government of Captain Ratcliffe, but only this discovery [*voyage*], wherein to express all the dangers, accidents, and encounters this small number passed in that small barge, by the scale of proportion—about three thousand miles [*more likely 2,000-2,500*], with such watery diet in those great waters and barbarous countries, till then to any Christian utterly unknown—I rather refer their merit to the censure of the courteous and experienced reader, than I would be tedious or partial being a party.

CHAPTER FIVE

President John Smith

September 10 to December 28, 1608

WHILE SMITH AND CREW *were off exploring, Ratcliffe had made a bid to regain his power and been imprisoned for mutiny. Though the summer had not been as hot as the previous year, many colonists had taken sick; several others had died. Much of the food had been spoiled by rain. The election on September 10 was a formality. Besides being one of the few surviving members of the Council, Smith was the only leader capable of keeping the colony from ruin. He took up the presidency with a will and began laying down the law. He would remain in Virginia for little more than a year, but during that time he would prove more effective than any Jamestown leader before or after.*

With orders from London always delayed by months at sea, Jamestown was the kind of outpost that needed a strong leader to survive. Smith was a natural for the role. Almost as soon as he had taken the helm, Newport arrived with a shipload of green colonists, including two women and eight "Dutchmen" (Germans) and Poles. And the same old orders—

find gold, a route to the South Sea, or a survivor of the Roanoke Colony. Furthermore, Newport was not to leave until one of these objectives had been accomplished. The Council in London also specified that Newport's verbal instructions must be strictly followed. In effect, Smith's authority was undercut, and he was indignant.

But by this time Smith knew better, and his main objective was to build up the strength of the colony. The Virginia Company seemed unaware that, after almost a year and a half, the survival of Jamestown was still not a given. Smith saw his responsibility as first to the colony and secondarily to the orders from London. Along with the Company's impractical orders, Newport had brought a barge in five pieces that was to be carried beyond the falls, assembled, and then taken happily on to whatever lay beyond (presumably, gold and the South Sea). And Newport had orders to conduct a coronation of Powhatan, a symbolic gesture probably meant to incorporate him into the English crown's authority.

Smith strongly objected to both of these plans, but he did his best to comply. Off he went to try to persuade Powhatan to come to Jamestown for the ceremony. While in Werowocomoco waiting for Powhatan's return, Smith and his men were treated by Pocohontas and a bevy of scantily clad young women to an altogether different kind of ceremony.

Powhatan refused to come to Jamestown for the ceremony; hence Newport and Smith headed a delegation to travel up the Pamunkey River. The Indian chief, naturally wary of the whole thing, was reluctant to kneel for his copper crown. Finally someone pushed him to his knees. A celebratory shot from the English boats made Powhatan jump in "horrible fear." Calm once again, Powhatan concluded the farce by presenting Newport with his old moccasins and deerskin mantle.

Back at the settlement, Newport attempted to undertake a journey up beyond the falls of the James. Even with 120 men, the five-piece barge was not transportable, and though the details of the trip are scanty, Smith's idea of burning the barge and carrying the ashes gives some sense of the men's frustration.

With Newport off on a pointless search for gold and silver, Smith went about trying to beef up the colony's nascent industrial works—the production of tar, pitch, glass, soap ashes, clapboard, and the like. Smith excelled in teaching men how to live and work out in the woods. His exuberant and creative leadership manifests itself here in a small but telling way when he punishes cursing and grumbling with an unusual method. One can imagine the whooping backwoods fraternalism that must have resulted.

Later in the fall, Smith had to bully the Chickahominy into trading for their corn. Ratcliffe and others, resenting his prowess, tried to depose him on the grounds that his methods with the Indians went against the letter of the instructions from London, which continued to advocate appeasement over threats. After a trumped-up charge that Smith had left his post without permission, the matter was dropped. In December, much to Smith's relief, Newport finally left, not having succeeded in his mission. But he took with him Smith's "Map of Chesapeake Bay and the River," along with an invaluable description of the geography and Indians and Smith's strongly worded letter to the King's Council for Virginia.

THE TENTH OF SEPTEMBER, by the election of the Council, and request of the company, Captain Smith received the letters patents, which till then by no means he would accept, though he was often importuned thereunto.

Now the building of Ratcliffe's palace stayed as a thing needless. The church was repaired, the storehouse recovered, buildings prepared for the supplies we expected, the fort reduced to a five-square form, the order of the watch renewed, the squadrons (each setting of the watch) trained.

The whole company every Saturday exercised in the plain by the west bulwark, prepared for that purpose, we called Smithfield, where sometimes more than a hundred savages would stand in an amazement to behold: how a file would batter a tree, where he would make them a mark to shoot at. The boats trimmed for trade, which being sent out with Lieutenant Percy, in their journey encountered the second supply, that brought them back to discover the country of Monacan.

How or why Captain Newport obtained such a private commission as not to return without a lump of gold, a certainty of the South Sea, or one of the lost company sent out by Sir Walter Raleigh, I know not; nor why he brought such a five-pieced barge, not to bear us to that South Sea till we had borne her over the mountains, which how far they extend is yet unknown.

As for the coronation of Powhatan, and his presents of basin and ewer [*pitcher*], bed, bedstead, clothes, and such costly novelties, they had been much better well spared than so ill spent. For we had his favor much better only for a plain piece of copper till this stately kind of soliciting made him so much overvalue himself that he respected us as much as nothing at all.

As for the hiring of the Poles and Dutchmen [*Deutsch, or Germans*] to make pitch, tar, glass, mills, and soap ashes, when the country is replenished with people and necessaries, would have done well. But to send them and 70 more without victuals to work was not so well advised nor considered of as it should have been. Yet this could not have hurt us had they been 200, though then we were 130 that wanted for ourselves. For we had the savages in that decorum, their harvest being newly gathered, that we feared not to get victuals for 500.

Now was there no way to make us miserable, but to neglect that time to make provision whilst it was to be had, the which was done [*anyway*] by the direction from England—to perform this strange discovery (but a more strange coronation), to lose that time, spend that victuals we had, tire and starve our men, having no means to carry victuals, munition, the hurt or sick, but on their own backs.

How or by whom they [*the orders*] were invented I know not. But Captain Newport we only accounted the author, who to effect these projects had so gilded men's hopes with great promises that both company and Council concluded his resolution for the most part. God doth know they little knew what they did, nor understood their own estates to conclude his conclusions, against all the inconveniences the foreseeing president alleged.

Of this supply [shipload] there was added to the Council one Captain Richard Waldo and Captain Winne, two ancient soldiers and valiant gentlemen, but yet ignorant of the business (being but newly arrived). Ratcliffe was also permitted to have his voice, and Master Scrivener desirous to see strange countries. So that although Smith was president, yet the major part of the Council had the authority and ruled it as they listed.

As for clearing Smith's objections—how pitch and tar, wainscot, clapboard, glass, and soap ashes could be provided, to relade the ship, or provision got to live withal when none was in the country (and that we had, spent before the ship departed to effect these projects), the answer was: Captain Newport undertook to freight the pinnace of 20 tons with corn in going and returning in his discovery [journey], and to refreight her again from Werowocomoco of Powhatan; also promising a great proportion of victuals from the ship, inferring that Smith's propositions were only devices to hinder his journey, to effect it himself, and that the cruelty he had used to the savages might well be the occasion to hinder these designs and seek revenge on him.

For which taxation all works were left, and 120 chosen men were appointed for Newport's guard in this discovery. But Captain Smith to make clear all those seeming suspicions—that the savages were not so desperate as was pretended by Captain Newport, and how willing (since by their authority they would have it so) he was to assist them what he could, because the coronation would consume much time—he undertook himself their message to Powhatan, to entreat him to come to Jamestown to receive his presents. And where Newport dare not go with less than 120, he only took with him Captain Waldo, Master Andrew Buckler, Edward Brinton, and Samuel Collier.

With these four he went overland to Werowocomoco, some 12 miles. There he passed the river of Pamunkey in a savage canoe. Powhatan, being 30 miles off, was presently sent for.

In the meantime, Pocahontas and her women entertained Captain Smith in this manner.

In a fair plain field they made a fire, before which, he sitting upon a mat, suddenly amongst the woods was heard such a hideous noise and shrieking that the English betook themselves to their arms and seized on two or three old men by them, supposing Powhatan with all his power was come to surprise them. But presently Pocahontas came, willing him to kill her if any hurt were intended, and the beholders, which were men, women, and children, satisfied the captain there was no such matter. Then presently they were presented with this antic: Thirty young women came naked out of the woods, only covered behind and before with a few green leaves, their bodies all painted, some of one color, some of another, but all differing. Their leader had a fair pair of buck's horns on her head, and an otter's skin at her girdle, and another at her arm, a quiver of arrows at her back, a bow and arrows in her hand. The next had in her hand a sword, another a club, another a pot stick, all horned alike; the rest every one with their several devices. These fiends with most hellish shouts and cries, rushing from among the trees, cast themselves in a ring about the fire, singing and dancing with most excellent ill variety, oft falling into their infernal passions, and solemnly again to sing and dance. Having spent near an hour in this masquerade, as they entered, in like manner they departed.

Having reaccommodated themselves, they solemnly invited him [Smith] to their lodgings, where he was no sooner within the house but all these nymphs more tormented him than ever, with crowding, pressing, and hanging about him, most tediously crying, "Love you not me? Love you not me?"

This salutation ended, the feast was set, consisting of all the savage dainties they could devise—some attending, others singing and dancing about them. Which mirth being ended, with firebrands instead of torches they conducted him to his lodging.

The next day came Powhatan. Smith delivered his message of the presents sent him—and redelivered him Namontack he had sent for England—desiring him to come to his father Newport, to accept those presents, and conclude their revenge against the Monacans. Whereunto this subtle savage thus replied:

"If your king have sent me presents, I also am a king, and this is my land. Eight days I will stay to receive them. Your father is to come to me, not I to him, nor yet to your fort; neither will I bite at such a bait. As for the Monacans, I can revenge my own injuries, and as for Atquanachuke, where you say your brother was slain, it is a contrary way from those parts you suppose it. But for any salt water beyond the mountains, the relations you have had from my people are false."

Whereupon he began to draw plots upon the ground (according to his discourse) of all those regions. Many other discourses they had (yet both content to give each other content in complementary courtesies), and so Captain Smith returned with this answer.

Upon this, Captain Newport sent his presents by water, which is near a hundred miles, and the captains went by land with fifty good shot.

All being met at Werowocomoco, the next day was appointed for his coronation. Then the presents were brought him, his basin and ewer, bed and furniture set up, his scarlet cloak and apparel with much ado put on him, being persuaded by Namontack they would not hurt him. But a foul trouble there was to make him kneel to receive his crown, he neither knowing the majesty nor meaning of

ENGRAVING OF POWHATAN ON SMITH'S 1612 MAP OF
VIRGINIA (WILLIAM HOLE, ENGRAVER)

a crown, nor bending of the knee; endured so many persuasions, examples, and instructions, as tired them all. At last by leaning hard on his shoulders, he a little stooped, and three having the crown in their hands put it on his head, when by the warning of a pistol the boats were prepared with such a volley of shot that the king started up in a horrible fear, till he saw all was well. Then, remembering himself, to congratulate their kindness he gave his old shoes and his mantle to Captain Newport.

But perceiving his purpose was to discover the Monacans, he labored to divert his resolution, refusing to lend him either men or guides more than Namontack. And so after some small complementary kindness on both sides, in requital of his presents he presented Newport with a heap of wheat ears that might contain some seven or eight bushels, and as much more we bought in the town, wherewith we returned to the fort.

The ship having unburdened herself of 70 persons, with the first gentlewoman and woman servant that arrived in our colony, Captain Newport with 120 chosen men—led by Captain Waldo, Lieutenant Percy, Captain Winne, Master West, and Master Scrivener—set forward for the discovery of Monacan, leaving the president at the fort with about 80 or 90 (such as they were) to relade the ship.

Arriving at the falls, we marched by land some forty miles in two days and a half, and so returned down the same path we went. Two towns we discovered of the Monacans, called Massinacack and Mowhemcho. The people neither used us well nor ill; yet for our security we took one of their petty kings, and led him bound to conduct us the way. And in our returns [we] searched many places we supposed mines, about which we spent some time in refining, having one William Callicut, a refiner fitted for that purpose. From that crust of earth we dug, he persuaded us to believe he extracted some small quantity of silver; and (not unlikely) better stuff might be had for the digging.

With this poor trial, being contented to leave this fair, fertile, well-watered country, and coming to the falls, the savages feigned there were divers ships come into the bay to kill them at Jamestown. Trade they would not, and find their corn we could not, for they had hid it in the woods. And being thus deluded, we arrived at Jamestown, half sick, all complaining, and tired with toil, famine, and discontent, to have only but discovered our gilded hopes, and such fruitless certainties, as Captain Smith foretold us.

No sooner were we landed but the president dispersed so many as were able—some for glass, others for tar, pitch, and soap ashes, leaving them with the fort to the Council's oversight. But 30 of us he conducted down the river some 5 miles from Jamestown to learn to make clapboard, cut down trees, and lie in woods. Amongst the rest he had chosen Gabriel Beadle and John Russell, the only two gallants of this last supply, and both proper gentlemen.

Strange were these pleasures to their conditions. Yet lodging, eating, and drinking, working or playing—they but doing as the president did himself—all these things were carried so pleasantly as within a week they became masters, making it their delight to hear the trees thunder as they fell. But the axes so often blistered their tender fingers that many times every third blow had a loud oath to drown the echo, for remedy of which sin the president devised how to have every man's oaths numbered, and at night for every oath to have a can of water poured down his sleeve, with which every offender was so washed (himself and all) that a man should scarce hear an oath in a week.

By this, let no man think that the president and these gentlemen spent their times as common wood haggers [hackers] at felling of trees, or such other like labors, or that they were pressed to it as hirelings, or common slaves. For what they did—after they were but once a little inured—it seemed, and some conceited it, only as a pleasure and recreation, yet 30 or 40 of such voluntary gentlemen would do more in a day than 100 of the rest that must be pressed to it by compulsion. But 20 good workmen had been better than them all.

Master Scrivener, Captain Waldo, and Captain Winne at the fort, every one in like manner carefully regarded their charge. The president returning from amongst the woods, seeing the time consumed and no provision gotten (and the ship lay idle at a great charge and did nothing), presently embarked himself in the discovery barge, giving order to the Council to send Lieutenant Percy after him with the next barge that arrived at the fort.

Two barges he had himself and 18 men, but arriving at Chickahamania that dogged nation was too well acquainted with our wants, refusing to trade, with as much scorn and insolence as they could express. The president perceiving it was Powhatan's policy to starve us, told them he came not so much for their corn, as to revenge his imprisonment and the death of his men murdered by them. And so landing his men and ready to charge them, they immediately fled, and presently after sent their ambassadors with corn, fish, fowl, and what they had to make their peace. Their corn being that year but bad, they complained extremely of their own wants, yet freighted our boats with a hundred bushels of corn, and in like manner Lieutenant Percy's that not long after arrived. And having done the best they could to content us, we parted good friends and returned to Jamestown.

Though this much contented the company, that feared nothing more than starving, yet some so envied his good success that they rather desired to hazard a starving than his pains should prove so much more effectual than theirs. Some projects there were invented by Newport and Ratcliffe, not only to have deposed him, but to have kept him out of the fort, for that being president, he would leave his place and the fort without their consents. But their horns were so much too short to effect it, as they themselves more narrowly escaped a greater mischief.

All this time our old tavern made as much of all them that had either money or ware as could be desired. By this time they were become so perfect on all sides (I mean the soldiers, sailors, and savages) as there was ten times more care to maintain their damnable and private trade than to provide for the colony things that were necessary. Neither was it a small policy in Newport and the mariners to report in England we had such plenty, and bring us so many men without victuals, when they had so many private factors [merchants] in the fort that within 6 or 7 weeks, of 200 or 300 axes, chisels, hoes, and pickaxes, scarce 20 could be found. And for pike-heads [pointed steel head of a long wooden weapon], shot, powder, or anything they could steal from their fellows was vendible. They knew as well (and as secretly) how to convey them to trade with the savages for furs, baskets, young beasts, or suchlike commodities, as exchange them with the sailors for butter, cheese, beef, pork, aqua vitae, beer, biscuit, oatmeal, and oil, and then feign all was sent them from their friends. And though Virginia afforded no furs for the store, yet one master in one voyage has got so many by this indirect means as he confessed to have sold in England for 30 pounds.

Those are the saint-seeming worthies of Virginia that have notwithstanding all this meat, drink, and wages, but now they begin to grow weary, their trade being both perceived and prevented. None has been in Virginia that has observed anything, which knows not this to be true; and yet the loss, the scorn, the misery, and shame, was the poor officers, gentlemen, and careless governors who were all thus bought and sold; the adventurers cozened, and the action overthrown by their false excuses, information, and directions. By this let all men judge how this business could prosper, being thus abused by such pilfering occasions. And had not Captain Newport cried "peccavi" [I have sinned], the president would have discharged the ship, and caused him to have stayed one year in Virginia, to learn to speak of his own experience.

Master Scrivener was sent with the barges and pinnace to Werowocomoco, where he found the savages more ready to fight than trade. But his vigilancy was such as prevented their projects, and by the means of Namontack got three or four hogsheads of corn and as much *pocones*, which is a red root which then was esteemed an excellent dye.

Captain Newport being dispatched with the trials of pitch, tar, glass, frankincense, soap ashes, with that clapboard and wainscot that could be provided, met with Master Scrivener at Point Comfort, and so returned for England. We remaining were about two hundred.

The Copy of a Letter sent to the Treasurer and Council of Virginia from Captain Smith, then President in Virginia:

> Right Honorable, etc.
>
> I received your letter, wherein you write that our minds are so set upon faction and idle conceits in dividing the country without your consents, and that we feed you but with ifs and ands, hopes, and some few proofs, as if we would keep the mystery of the business to ourselves, and that we must expressly follow your instructions sent by Captain Newport, the charge of whose voyage amounts to near two thousand pounds, the which if we cannot defray by the ship's return, we are like to remain as banished men. To these particulars I humbly entreat your pardons if I offend you with my rude answer.
>
> For our factions, unless you would have me run away and leave the country, I cannot prevent them because I do make many stay that would else fly any whither. For the idle letter sent to my Lord of Salisbury by the president [*Ratcliffe*] and his confederates, for dividing the country, etc.: What it was I know not, for you saw no hand of mine to it, nor ever dreamed I of any such matter.
>
> That we feed you with hopes, etc., though I be no scholar, I am past a schoolboy, and I desire but to know what either you

and these here do know, but that I have learned to tell you by the continual hazard of my life. I have not concealed from you anything I know, but I fear some cause you to believe much more than is true.

Expressly to follow your directions by Captain Newport, though they be performed, I was directly against it. But according to our commission, I was content to be overruled by the major part of the Council, I fear to the hazard of us all; which now is generally confessed when it is too late. Only Captain Winne and Captain Waldo I have sworn of the Council, and crowned Powhatan according to your instructions.

For the charge of this voyage of two or three thousand pounds, we have not received the value of a hundred pounds. And for the quartered boat to be born by the soldiers over the falls, Newport had 120 of the best men he could choose. If he had burned her to ashes, one might have carried her in a bag—but as she is, five hundred cannot, to a navigable place above the falls.

And for him at that time to find in the South Sea, a mine of gold, or any of them sent by Sir Walter Raleigh, at our consultation I told them was as likely as the rest. But during this "great discovery" of 30 miles (which might as well have been done by one man, and [made] much more for the value of a pound of copper at a seasonable time), they had the pinnace and all the boats with them but one that remained with me to serve the fort.

In their absence I followed the new begun works of pitch and tar, glass, soap ashes, and clapboard, whereof some small quantities we have sent you. But if you rightly consider what an infinite toil it is in Russia and Swethland [Sweden], where the woods are proper for naught else, and though there be the help both of man and beast in those ancient commonwealths, which many a hundred years have used it, yet thousands of those poor people can scarce get necessaries to live but from hand to mouth. And though your factors there can buy as much in a week as will freight you a ship, or as much as you please, you must not expect from us any such matter, which are but a many of ignorant miserable souls that are scarce able to get wherewith to live and defend ourselves against the inconstant savages, finding but here and there a tree fit for the purpose, and want all things else the Russians have.

For the coronation of Powhatan: By whose advice you sent him such presents I know not. But this give me leave to tell you. I fear they will be the confusion of us all ere we hear from you again. At your ship's arrival, the savages' harvest was newly gathered, and we going to buy it, our own not being half sufficient for so great a number. As for the two ships loading of corn Newport promised to provide us from Powhatan, he brought us but fourteen bushels, and from the Monacans nothing, but the most of the men sick and near famished. From your ship we had not provision in victuals worth 20 pounds, and we are more than 200 to live upon this—the one half sick, the other little better.

For the sailors, I confess, they daily make good cheer, but our diet is a little meal and water, and not sufficient of that. Though there be fish in the sea, fowls in the air, and beasts in the woods, their bounds are so large, they so wild, and we so weak and ignorant, we cannot much trouble them. Captain Newport we much suspect to be the author of those inventions [reports].

Now that you should know, I have made you as great a discovery as he, for less charge than he spends you every meal. I have sent you this map of the bay and rivers, with an annexed relation of the countries and nations that inhabit them, as you may see at large. Also two barrels of stones, and such as I take to be good iron ore at the least, so divided as by their notes you may see in what places I found them.

The soldiers say many of your officers maintain their families out of that you send us, and that Newport has a hundred pounds a year for carrying news. For every master you have yet sent can find the way as well as he, so that a hundred pounds might be spared, which is more than we have all, that help to pay him wages.

Captain Ratcliffe is now called Sicklemore, a poor counterfeited impostor. I have sent you him home, lest the company should cut his throat. What he is now, everyone can tell you. If he and Archer return again, they are sufficient to keep us always in factions. When you send again I entreat you rather send but thirty carpenters, husbandmen, gardeners, fishermen, blacksmiths, masons, and diggers up of trees, roots, well provided, than a thousand of such as we have. For except we be able both to lodge them, and feed them, the most will consume with want of necessaries before they can be made good for anything.

Thus if you please to consider this account, and of the unnecessary wages to Captain Newport, or his ships so long lingering and staying here (for notwithstanding his boasting to leave us victuals for 12 months, though we had 89 by this discovery lame and sick, and but a pint of corn a day for a man, we were constrained to give him three hogsheads of that to victual him homeward), or yet to send into Germany or Poland for glassmen and the rest, till we be able to sustain ourselves and relieve them when they come.

It were better to give 500 pounds a ton for those gross commodities in Denmark than send for them hither, till more necessary things be provided. For in overtoiling our weak and unskillful bodies to satisfy this desire of present profit, we can scarce ever recover ourselves from one supply to another. And I humbly entreat you hereafter, let us know what we should receive, and not stand to the sailors courtesy to leave us what they please, else you may charge us with what you will, but we not you with anything. These are the causes that have kept us in Virginia from laying such a foundation that ere this might have given much better content and satisfaction. But as yet you must not look for any profitable returns. So I humbly rest.

EARLY JAMESTOWN SETTLERS TRADING WITH
NATIVE AMERICANS (1619)

These poor conclusions so affrighted us all with famine that
the president provided for Nansemond and took with him Captain
Winne and Master Scrivener, then returning from Captain Newport [*from escorting him downriver*].

These people also long denied him not only the 400 baskets of
corn they promised, but any trade at all—excusing themselves they
had spent most they had and were commanded by Powhatan to
keep that they had and not to let us come into their river, till we
were constrained to begin with them perforce.

Upon the discharging of our muskets they all fled and shot not
an arrow. The first house we came to we set on fire, which when
they perceived, they desired we would make no more spoil and
they would give us half they had. How they collected it I know not,

but before night they loaded our three boats. And so we returned to our quarters some four miles down the river, which was only the open woods under the lay of a hill, where all the ground was covered with snow and hard frozen. The snow we dug away and made a great fire in the place; when the ground was well dried, we turned away the fire and, covering the place with a mat, there we lay very warm. To keep us from the wind we made a shade of another mat; as the wind turned we turned our shade, and when the ground grew cold we removed the fire. And thus many a cold winter night have we lain in this miserable manner, yet those that most commonly went upon all those occasions were always in health, lusty, and fat.

For sparing them this year, the next year they promised to plant purposely for us; and so loading our boats with 100 bushels, we parted good friends and we returned to Jamestown.

About this time there was a marriage betwixt John Laydon and Anne Burras, which was the first marriage we had in Virginia.

Long he [Smith] stayed not, but fitting himself and Captain Waldo with two barges. From Chawopo, Weanoc, and all parts thereabouts, all the people were fled, as being jealous of our intents, till we discovered the river and people of Appomattoc, where we found not much. That they had we equally divided, but gave them copper and such things as contented them in consideration. Master Scrivener and Lieutenant Percy went also abroad, but could find nothing.

The president seeing the procrastinating of time was no course to live, resolved with Captain Waldo (whom he knew to be sure in time of need) to surprise Powhatan and all his provision. But the unwillingness of Captain Winne and Master Scrivener, for some private respect, plotted in England to ruin Captain Smith, did their best to hinder their project. [Scrivener, formerly Smith's protégé, decides now that Smith's idea of a surprise attack on Powhatan is not a good idea. Smith abandons the plan.]

But the president, whom no persuasions could persuade to starve, being invited by Powhatan to come unto him—and if he would send him but men to build him a house, give him a grindstone, fifty swords, some pieces, a cock, and a hen, with much copper and beads—he would load his ship with corn. The president not ignorant of his devices and subtlety, yet unwilling to neglect any opportunity, presently sent three Dutchmen and two English. Having so small allowance, few were able to do anything to purpose. Knowing there needed no better a castle [house] to effect this project, [Smith] took order with Captain Waldo to second him, if need required. Scrivener he left his substitute, and set forth with the pinnace, two barges, and forty-six, which only were such as voluntarily offered themselves for his journey, the which by reason of Master Scrivener's ill success was censured [deemed] very desperate, they all knowing Smith would not return empty if it were to be had. Howsoever, it caused many of those that he had appointed to find excuses to stay behind.

CHAPTER SIX

Powhatan the Subtle Savage

December 29, 1608, to February 1609

THE NEW ORDERS FROM LONDON *seemed to Smith an attempt to appease the Powhatans, and he began finding the Indians much more difficult to deal with. When Newport left in December, Smith went right back to his old policy of iron-fisted diplomacy. By cajoling and bullying he was usually able to get what he wanted from the Indians without any bloodshed. But his strong-arm, sometimes brutal, tactics inevitably did lead to skirmishes, casualties, and ill will on both sides. Generally he used the same feudal techniques he used on the bay expeditions: demand tribute (in the form of food and weapons) from a village, while threatening to destroy it; afterwards reward the villagers with trinkets.*

But it was clear by late December that the local Indians had decided to simply let the colony starve rather than do business with them. There were now about 200 colonists, 30 of them from the first shipment. The mortality rate had declined from over 60 percent to under 20 percent, but food was still in short supply and a bad winter could doom the colony. The colonists each needed a pint of corn a day. Powhatan finally offered to trade with the English if they would send him some workmen to build an English-style house; he also wanted a grindstone, guns, swords, chickens, copper, and glass beads.

On December 29 Smith and a party of 50 men set out by boat and foot to Werowocomoco, to get food from Powhatan. The Pamunkey River was a frozen ooze, and the crews had to break ice to get to the chief's village. They arrived on January 12. Powhatan complained that he did not have all the corn the English wanted, but he could spare 40 baskets for 40 swords. Smith harangued him: "As for swords and guns, I told you long ago I had none to spare." The two leaders, both respectful of the other's shrewdness, went back and forth, reminding each other of their mutual promises. Powhatan's reply rings today as a particularly stinging rebuke: "What will it avail you to take that by force you may quickly have by love?" From Smith's point of view, Powhatan was simply making another chess move.

A shadowy subplot involving the Dutchmen and Poles began around this time. Smith sent one to Powhatan's camp to scope out the situation before his own party arrived. The man became a counterspy and began working for Powhatan, as did his countrymen, who were sent to help build Powhatan's house. They apparently let Powhatan understand that they were ultimately on his side should things go bad for the colony, which was Powhatan's greatest wish. Seeing their usefulness, Powhatan kept them around.

Pocahontas became a major player in the power struggle between Powhatan and Smith. The chief's adolescent daughter had a fondness amounting to a crush on the much older captain, and she was fascinated by the strange life of the fort, with its odd animals, gadgets, and people—the horses, cows, mirrors, iron kettles, woven cloths, buildings, and foreign language. It was like a circus to which she, with a supple, curious mind, could not but be attracted. Not long after the parley at Werowocomoco, she risked her life to come one night and warn Smith of a plot against him.

Powhatan then sent two of his counterspies to Jamestown to gather a supply of arms for the Indians of Werowocomoco. Smith in the meantime

C. Smith taketh the King of Pamavnkee prisoner. -1608.

Smith seizes Opechancanough by the hair
(*General History*, 1624).

had made it to Opechancanough's headquarters 25 miles up the Pamunkey River from Werowocomoco, where he proceeded to barter for corn. But shortly the English were surrounded by hundreds of Indians. Cornered, Smith offered to battle Opechancanough man-to-man. The elderly chief said he had not intended any harm. Still suspecting a trap, Smith grabbed him by his scalp lock and pointed a pistol at his chest. Pulling his terrified hostage into a crowd of Indians, Smith gave a fiery oration (probably insane-sounding to the Indians). The result was that they loaded his boat with corn and supplies. Unfortunately, the humiliation of

Opechancanough, successor to Powhatan, would rankle for the rest of his long life. The expedient of obtaining food would have repercussions long after Smith had gone.

Just after the scene with Opechancanough, Smith received word that Scrivener, Waldo, Anthony Gosnold, and eight others had boated over to Hog Island near Jamestown and turned up dead, presumably the boat overturning in a wind. Why they went is unknown, and no one seemed to know exactly how they died. In the following days, the tension eased somewhat, with some Indians, ever fearful of Smith, gathering all the corn they could, and others trying to find ways to destroy him. After a failed ambush, an attempt to poison him left him sick to his stomach.

Despite Smith's heroic efforts to hold things together, the executives across the Atlantic were not pleased. They were dissatisfied with the return on their investment—there was as yet no mineral wealth, nor a passage to the East. And they thought Smith's tough approach to the Indians was altogether the wrong way to get what the colony wanted.

Smith was disgusted with these breezy assessments from people who had no idea what the situation was really like on Virginia soil. And as for the mineral wealth that the Spanish seemed to find easily in South America—well, the English simply had bad luck. If Virginia had been peopled by a more advanced civilization, Smith observed, "adorned with such store of precious jewels and rich commodities as was the Indies," it would be different. "But we chanced in a land even as God made it." Today that sounds like a wilderness paradise, but 400 years ago it was too common to be of value.

THE TWENTY-NINE OF DECEMBER he set forward for Werowocomoco; his company were these:

In the discovery barge himself.

Gentlemen
Robert Beheathland.

Raleigh Chrashow.
Nathaniel Powell.
Michael Sicklemore.
John Russell.
Richard Worley.

Soldiers
Anas Todkill.
Jeffrey Shortridge.
William Love.
Edward Pising.
William Bentley.
William Ward.

In the pinnace.
Lieutenant Percy, *brother to the Earl of Northumberland.*
Master Francis West, *brother to the Lord La Warr.*
William Phettiplace, *Captain of the pinnace.*

Gentlemen
Michael Phettiplace.
Jeffrey Abbot, *Sergeant.*
William Tankard.
George Yarington.
Jonas Profit, *Master.*
Robert Ford, *Clerk of the Council.*

Soldiers.
Anthony Bagnall.
James Bourne.
Edward Brinton.
George Burton.

Thomas Coe.

John Dods.

Henry Powell.

Thomas Gipson, David Ellis, Nathaniel Peacock, *Sailors*. John Prat, George Acrig, James Read, Nicholas Hancock, James Watkins, Thomas Lambert, four Dutchmen, and Richard Savage were sent by land before to build the house for Powhatan against our arrival.

This company being victualed but for three or four days, lodged the first night at Warraskoyack, where the president took sufficient provision. This kind king did his best to divert him from seeing Powhatan, but perceiving he could not prevail, he advised in this manner.

"Captain Smith, you shall find Powhatan to use you kindly, but trust him not, and be sure he have no opportunity to seize on your arms, for he hath sent for you only to cut your throats."

The captain thanking him for his good counsel, yet the better to try his love, desired guides to Chawanoac; for he would send a present to that king to bind him his friend. To perform this journey was sent Master Sicklemore [*no relation to Ratcliffe*], a very valiant, honest, and a painful soldier, with him two guides and directions how to seek for the lost company of Sir Walter Raleigh's and silk grass.

Then we departed thence, the president assuring the king perpetual love, and left with him Samuel Collier his page to learn the language.

The next night being lodged at Kecoughtan, six or seven days the extreme wind, rain, frost, and snow caused us to keep Christmas among the savages, where we were never more merry, nor fed on more plenty of good oysters, fish, flesh, wildfowl, and good bread;

nor never had better fires in England than in the dry smoky houses of Kecoughtan. But departing thence, when we found no houses, we were not curious in any weather to lie three or four nights together under the trees by a fire as formerly is said.

An hundred forty-eight fowls the president, Anthony Bagnall, and Sergeant Pising did kill at three shoots. At Kiskiack the frost and contrary winds forced us three or four days also (to suppress the insolence of those proud savages) to quarter in their houses, yet guard our barge, and cause them give us what we wanted, though we were but twelve and himself. Yet we never wanted shelter where we found any houses.

The 12 of January [1609] we arrived at Werowocomoco, where the river was frozen near half a mile from the shore. But to neglect no time, the president with his barge so far had approached by breaking the ice, as the ebb left him amongst those oozy shoals. Yet rather than to lie there frozen to death, by his own example he taught them to march near middle deep, a flightshot [bowshot] through this muddy frozen oasis.

When the barge floated, he appointed two or three to return her aboard the pinnace. Where for want of water in melting the ice, they made fresh water, for the river there was salt. But in this march Master Russell (whom none could persuade to stay behind) being somewhat ill and exceedingly heavy, so overtoiled himself as the rest had much ado (ere he got ashore) to regain life into his dead benumbed spirits.

Quartering in the next houses we found, we sent to Powhatan for provision, who sent us plenty of bread, turkeys, and venison. The next day having feasted us after his ordinary manner, he began to ask us when we would be gone, feigning he sent not for us, neither had he any corn and his people much less; yet for forty swords he would procure us forty baskets. The president showing him the men there present that brought him the message and conditions asked Powhatan how it chanced he became so forgetful. Thereat the king concluded the matter with a merry laughter, asking for our commodities, but none he liked without guns and swords, valuing a basket of corn more precious than a basket of copper, saying he could eat his corn, but not the copper.

Captain Smith, seeing the intent of this subtle savage began to deal with him after this manner:

"Powhatan, though I had many courses to have made my provision, yet believing your promises to supply my wants, I neglected all to satisfy your desire. And to testify my love, I send you my men for your building, neglecting mine own. What your people had you have engrossed, forbidding them our trade. And now you think by consuming the time, we shall consume for want, not having to fulfill your strange demands. As for swords and guns, I told you long ago I had none to spare, and you must know those I have can keep me from want. Yet steal or wrong you I will not, nor dissolve that friendship we have mutually promised, except you constrain me by our bad usage."

The king having attentively listened to this discourse, promised that both he and his country would spare him what he could, the which within two days they should receive.

"Yet Captain Smith," sayeth the king, "some doubt I have of your coming hither, that makes me not so kindly seek to relieve you as I would. For many do inform me your coming hither is not for trade, but to invade my people and possess my country, who dare not come to bring you corn, seeing you thus armed with your men. To free us of this fear, leave aboard your weapons, for here they are needless, we being all friends and forever Powhatans."

With many such discourses they spent the day, quartering that night in the king's houses.

The next day he renewed his building, which he little intended should proceed. For the Dutchmen finding his plenty, and

Palisaded Indian village with longhouses (Theodor de Bry, 1590
engraving, based on a watercolor from the Roanoke colony)

knowing our want, and perceiving his preparations to surprise
us—little thinking we could escape both him and famine—to
obtain his favor revealed to him so much as they knew of our
estates and projects, and how to prevent them. One of them
being of so great a spirit, judgment, and resolution, and a hireling
that was certain of his wages for his labor, and ever well used
both he and his countrymen that the president knew not whom
better to trust, and not knowing any fitter for that employment,
had sent him as a spy to discover Powhatan's intent, then little
doubting his honesty, nor could ever be certain of his villainy till
near half a year after.

Whilst we expected the coming in of the country, we wrangled out of the king ten quarters of corn for a copper kettle, the which the president perceiving him much to affect, valued it at a much greater rate. But in regard of his scarcity he would accept it, provided we should have as much more the next year, or else the country of Monacan. Wherewith each seemed well contented, and Powhatan began to expostulate the difference of peace and war after this manner:

"Captain Smith, you may understand that I having seen the death of all my people thrice, and not anyone living of those three generations but myself, I know the difference of peace and war better than any in my country. But now I am old and ere long must die. My brethren, namely Opitchapam, Opechancanough, and Kekataugh, my two sisters, and their two daughters, are distinctly each other's successors. I wish their experience no less than mine, and your love to them no less than mine to you.

"But this bruit from Nansemond that you are come to destroy my country so much affrighteth all my people as they dare not visit you. What will it avail you to take that by force you may quickly have by love, or to destroy them that provide you food? What can you get by war, when we can hide our provisions and fly to the woods, whereby you must famish by wronging us your friends? And why are you thus jealous of our loves seeing us unarmed, and both do and are willing still to feed you, with that you cannot get but by our labors?

"Think you I am so simple, not to know it is better to eat good meat, lie well, and sleep quietly with my women and children, laugh and be merry with you, have copper, hatchets, or what I want being your friend than be forced to fly from all, to lie cold in the woods, feed upon acorns, roots, and such trash, and be so hunted by you that I can neither rest, eat, nor sleep? But my tired men must watch, and if a twig but break, everyone cryeth, 'There cometh Captain

Smith!' Then must I fly I know not whither and thus with miserable fear, end my miserable life, leaving my pleasures to such youths as you, which through your rash unadvisedness may quickly as miserably end, for want of that you never know where to find.

"Let this therefore assure you of our loves, and every year our friendly trade shall furnish you with corn. And now also, if you would come in friendly manner to see us, and not thus with your guns and swords as to invade your foes."

To this subtle discourse, the president thus replied.

"Seeing you will not rightly conceive of our words, we strive to make you know our thoughts by our deeds. The vow I made you of my love, both myself and my men have kept. As for your promise, I find it every day violated by some of your subjects. Yet we finding your love and kindness, our custom is so far from being ungrateful that for your sake only, we have curbed our thirsting desire of revenge, else had they known as well the cruelty we use to our enemies, as our true love and courtesy to our friends. And I think your judgment sufficient to conceive—as well by the adventures we have undertaken as by the advantage we have (by our arms) of yours—that had we intended you any hurt, long ere this we could have effected it.

"Your people coming to Jamestown are entertained with their bows and arrows without any exceptions. We esteeming it with you as it is with us to wear our arms as our apparel. As for the danger of our enemies, in such wars consist our chiefest pleasure. For your riches we have no use. As for the hiding your provision, or by your flying to the woods, we shall not so unadvisedly starve as you conclude. Your friendly care in that behalf is needless, for we have a rule to find beyond your knowledge."

Many other discourses they had, till at last they began to trade. But the king seeing his will would not be admitted as a law, our guard dispersed, nor our men disarmed, he (sighing) breathed his mind once more in this manner.

"Captain Smith, I never use any werowance so kindly as your-self, yet from you I receive the least kindness of any. Captain Newport gave me swords, copper, clothes, a bed, tools, or what I desired, ever taking what I offered him, and would send away his guns when I entreated him. None doth deny to lie at my feet, or refuse to do what I desire, but only you, of whom I can have nothing but what you regard not. And yet you will have whatso-ever you demand. Captain Newport you call father, and so you call me, but I see for all us both you will do what you list, and we must both seek to content you. But if you intend so friendly as you say, send hence your arms that I may believe you, for you see the love I bear you doth cause me thus nakedly to forget myself." [*Smith unabashedly reports Powhatan's response to his own hard-nosed bargaining, in contrast to Newport's softer manner. First published in 1612, Smith's account came out shortly after events in Jamestown proved Smith's policy sounder than Newport's. Shortly after Smith's departure in 1610, Jamestown's fortunes plummeted.*]

Smith seeing this savage but trifle the time to cut his throat, pro-cured the savages to break the ice that his boat might come to fetch his corn and him, and gave order for more men to come on shore to surprise the king, with whom also he but trifled the time till his men were landed, and to keep him from suspicion entertained the time with this reply.

"Powhatan you must know, as I have but one God, I honor but one king. And I live not here as your subject, but as your friend to pleasure you with what I can. By the gifts you bestow on me, you gain more than by trade. Yet would you visit me as I do you, you should know it is not our custom to sell our courtesies as a vendible commodity. Bring all your country with you for your guard; I will not dislike it as being over jealous. But to content you, tomorrow I will leave my arms and trust to your promise. I call you father indeed, and as a father you shall see I will love you. But the small care you have of such a child caused my men to persuade me to look to myself."

By this time Powhatan having knowledge his men were ready whilst the ice was a-breaking, with his luggage, women, and children, fled. Yet to avoid suspicion, left two or three of the women talking with the captain, whilst he secretly ran away, and his men that secretly beset the house. Which being presently discovered to Captain Smith, with his pistol, sword, and target he made such a passage among these naked devils, that at his first shoot they next him tumbled one over another, and the rest quickly fled some one way some another. So that without any hurt, only accompanied with John Russell, he obtained the *corps du guard.*

When they perceived him so well escaped, and with his eighteen men (for he had no more with him ashore) to the uttermost of their skill they sought excuses to dissemble the matter, and Powhatan to excuse his flight and the sudden coming of this multitude sent our captain a great bracelet and a chain of pearl by an ancient orator that bespoke us to this purpose, perceiving even then from our pinnace a barge and men departing and coming unto us.

"Captain Smith, our werowance is fled, fearing your guns, and knowing when the ice was broken there would come more men, sent these numbers but to guard his corn from stealing that might happen without your knowledge. Now though some be hurt by your misprision, yet Powhatan is your friend and so will forever continue. Now since the ice is open, he would have you send away your corn, and if you would have his company, send away also your guns, which so affright his people that they dare not come to you as he promised they should."

Then having provided baskets for our men to carry our corn to the boats, they kindly offered their service to guard our arms that

none should steal them. A great many they were of goodly well proportioned fellows, as grim as devils. Yet the very sight of cocking
our matches, and being to let fly, a few words caused them to leave
their bows and arrows to our guard and bear down our corn on
their backs. We needed not importune them to make dispatch. But
our barges being left on the oasis by the ebb, caused us stay till the
next high water, so that we returned again to our old quarter.

Powhatan and his Dutchmen bursting with desire to have the
head of Captain Smith, for if they could but kill him they thought
all was theirs, neglected not any opportunity to effect his purpose.
The Indians with all the merry sports they could devise, spent the
time till night. Then they all returned to Powhatan, who all this
time was making ready his forces to surprise the house and him
at supper. Notwithstanding the eternal all-seeing God did prevent
him, and by a strange means.

For Pocahontas his dearest jewel and daughter, in that dark
night came through the irksome woods, and told our captain great
cheer should be sent us by and by. But Powhatan and all the power
he could make, would after come kill us all, if they that brought
it could not kill us with our own weapons when we were at supper. Therefore if we would live she wished us presently to be gone.
Such things as she delighted in he would have given her, but with
the tears running down her cheeks she said she dared not be seen
to have any. For if Powhatan should know it, she were but dead, and
so she ran away by herself as she came.

Within less than an hour came eight or ten lusty fellows, with
great platters of venison and other victual, very importunate to
have us put out our matches (whose smoke made them sick) and
sit down to our victual. But the captain made them taste every
dish, which done he sent some of them back to Powhatan to bid
him make haste, for he was prepared for his coming. As for them
he knew they came to betray him at his supper, but he would

prevent them and all their other intended villainies, so that they might be gone.

Not long after came more messengers, to see what news; not long after them, others. Thus we spent the night as vigilantly as they, till it was high water, yet seemed to the savages as friendly as they to us, and that we were so desirous to give Powhatan content, as he requested, we did leave him Edward Brinton to kill him fowl, and the Dutchmen to finish his house, thinking at our return from Pamunkey the frost would be gone, and then we might find a better opportunity if necessity did occasion it, little dreaming yet of the Dutchmen's treachery, whose humor well suited this verse.

Is any free that may not live as freely as he list?
Let us live so, then we are as free and brutish as the best.
—Persius

We had no sooner set sail but Powhatan returned, and sent Adam and Francis (two stout Dutchmen) to Jamestown, who feigning to Captain Winne that all things were well and that Captain Smith had use of their arms, wherefore they requested new (the which were given them). They told him their coming was for some extraordinary tools and shift of apparel, by which colorable excuse they obtained six or seven more to their confederacy—such expert thieves that presently furnished them with a great many swords, pike-heads, pieces, shot, powder, and suchlike savages they had at hand to carry it away.

And the next day they returned unsuspected, leaving their confederates to follow, and in the interim to convey them such things as they could, for which service they should live with Powhatan as his chief affected, free from those miseries that would happen [to] the colony.

Samuel their other consort Powhatan kept for their pledge, whose diligence had provided them three hundred of their kind of hatchets, the rest fifty swords, eight pieces, and eight pikes. Brinton and Richard Savage, seeing the Dutchmen so diligent to accommodate the savages with weapons, attempted to have gotten to Jamestown, but they were apprehended and expected ever when to be put to death.

Within two or three days we arrived at Pamunkey. The king as many days entertained us with feasting and much mirth. And the day appointed to begin our trade, the president, Lieutenant Percy, Master West, Master Russell, Master Beheathland, Master Crashaw, Master Powell, Master Ford, and some others to the number of fifteen went up to Opechancanough's house a quarter of a mile from the river, where we found nothing but a lame fellow and a boy. And all the houses round about of all things abandoned. Not long we stayed ere the king arrived, and after him came diverse of his people loaded with bows and arrows, but such pinching commodities, and those esteemed at such a value, as our captain began with the king after this manner.

"Opechancanough, the great love you profess with your tongue seems mere deceit by your actions. Last year you kindly freighted our ship, but now you have invited me to starve with hunger. You know my want, and I your plenty—of which by some means I must have part. Remember, it is fit for kings to keep their promise. Here are my commodities, whereof take your choice; the rest I will proportion fit bargains for your people."

The king seemed kindly to accept his offer, and the better to color his project, sold us what they had to our own content, promising the next day more company, better provided. The barges and pinnace being committed to the charge of Master Phettiplace, the president with his old fifteen marched up to the king's house, where we found four or five men newly arrived, each with a great basket. Not long after came the king, who with a strained cheerfulness held us with discourse what pains he had taken to keep his promise, till Master Russell brought us in news that we were all betrayed. For at least seven hundred savages [*an exaggeration, according to Barbour*] well armed had environed the house and beset the fields. The king conjecturing what Russell related, we could well perceive how the extremity of his fear betrayed his intent. Whereat some of our company seeming dismayed with the thought of such a multitude, the captain encouraged us to this effect.

"Worthy countrymen, were the mischiefs of my seeming friends no more than the danger of these enemies, I little cared were they as many more. If you dare, do but as I. But this is my torment, that if I escape them, our malicious Council with their openmouthed minions will make me such a peace-breaker (in their opinions in England) as will break my neck. I could wish those here that make these seem saints, and me an oppressor. But this is the worst of all, wherein I pray you aid me with your opinions.

"Should we begin with them and surprise the king, we cannot keep him and defend well ourselves. If we should each kill our man, and so proceed with all in the house, the rest will all fly. Then shall we get no more than the bodies that are slain, and so starve for victual. As for their fury it is the least danger. For well you know, being alone assaulted with two or three hundred of them, I made them by the help of God compound to save my life. And we are sixteen, and they but seven hundred at the most. And assure yourselves, God will so assist us that if you dare stand but to discharge your pieces, the very smoke will be sufficient to affright them. Yet howsoever, let us fight like men, and not die like sheep. For by that means you know God hath oft delivered me, and so I trust will now. But first, I will deal with them, to bring it to pass we may fight for something, and draw them to it by conditions. If you like this motion, promise me you will be valiant."

The time not permitting any argument, all vowed to execute whatsoever he attempted, or die. Whereupon the captain in plain terms told the king this.

"I see, Opechancanough, your plot to murder me, but I fear it not. As yet your men and mine have done no harm, but by our direction. Take therefore your arms; you see mine. My body shall be as naked as yours. The isle in your river is a fit place, if you be contented; and the conqueror (of us two) shall be lord and master over all our men. If you have not enough, take time to fetch more, and bring what number you will, so every one bring a basket of corn, against all which I will stake the value in copper. You see I have but fifteen, and our game shall be the conqueror take all."

The king being guarded with forty or fifty of his chief men, seemed kindly to appease Smith's suspicion of unkindness by a great present at the door they entreated him to receive. This was to draw him out of the door, where the bait was guarded with at least two hundred men, and thirty lying under a great tree (that lay athwart as a barricade), each his arrow nocked ready to shoot.

The president commanded one to go see what kind of deceit this was, and to receive the present, but he refused to do it. Yet the gentlemen and all the rest were importunate to go, but he would not permit them, being vexed at that coward, and commanded Lieutenant Percy, Master West, and the rest to make good the house. Master Powell and Master Beheathland he commanded to guard the door, and in such a rage snatched the king by his long lock in the midst of his men, with his pistol ready bent against his breast. Thus he led the trembling king, near dead with fear amongst all his people, who delivering the captain his vambrace [forearm armor], bow, and arrows, all his men were easily entreated to cast down their arms, little dreaming any dared in that manner have used their king, who then to escape himself bestowed his presents in good sadness. And causing a great many of them come before him unarmed, holding the king by the hair (as is said), he spoke to them to this effect.

"I see, you Pamunkeys, the great desire you have to kill me. And my long suffering your injuries hath emboldened you to this presumption. The cause I have forborne your insolences is the promise I made you (before the God I serve) to be your friend, till you give me just cause to be your enemy. If I keep this vow, my God will keep me; you cannot hurt me. If I break it, he will destroy me. But if you shoot but one arrow to shed one drop of blood of any of my men, or steal the least of these beads or copper I spurn here before you with my foot, you shall see I will not cease revenge (if once I begin) so long as I can hear where to find one of your nation that will not deny the name of Pamunkey.

"I am not now at Rassawek half drowned with mire, where you took me prisoner. Yet then for keeping your promise and your good usage and saving my life, I so affect you that your denials of your treachery do half persuade me to mistake myself. But if I be the mark you aim at, here I stand. Shoot he that dare. You promised to freight my ship ere I departed, and so you shall, or I mean to load her with your dead carcasses. Yet if as friends you will come and trade, I once more promise not to trouble you, except you give me the first occasion. And your king shall be free and be my friend, for I am not come to hurt him or any of you."

Upon this away went their bows and arrows, and men, women, and children brought in their commodities. Two or three hours they so thronged about the president and so overwearied him, as he retired himself to rest, leaving Master Beheathland and Master Powell to receive their presents. But some savages perceiving him fast asleep, and the guard somewhat carelessly dispersed, forty or fifty of their choice men each with a club, or an English sword in his hand began to enter the house with two or three hundred others, that pressed to second them.

The noise and haste they made in did so shake the house they awoke him from his sleep, and being half amazed with this sudden sight, betook him straight to his sword and target. Master Crashaw and some others charged in like manner; whereat they quickly thronged faster back than before forward. The house thus cleansed, the king and some of his ancients we kept yet with him, who with a long oration, excused this intrusion.

The rest of the day was spent with much kindness, the company again renewing their presents with their best provisions, and whatsoever he gave them they seemed therewith well contented.

Now in the meanwhile since our departure, this happened at our fort. Master Scrivener having received letters from England to make himself either "Caesar or nothing," he began to decline in his affection to Captain Smith, that ever regarded him as himself, and was willing to cross the surprising of Powhatan.

Some certain days [nine] after the president's departure, he [Scrivener] would needs go visit the Isle of Hogs, and took with him Captain Waldo (though the president had appointed him to be ready to second his occasions) with Master Anthony Gosnold and eight others. But so violent was the wind (that extreme frozen time) that the boat sunk, but where or how none doth know. The skiff was much overloaded, and would scarce have lived in that extreme tempest had she been empty. But by no persuasion he could be diverted, though both Waldo and a hundred others doubted as it happened. The savages were the first that found their bodies, which so much the more encouraged them to effect their projects.

To advertise the president of this heavy news, none could be found would undertake it. But the journey was often refused of all in the fort, until Master Richard Wiffin undertook alone the performance thereof.

In this journey he was encountered with many dangers and difficulties in all parts as he passed. As for that night he lodged with Powhatan, perceiving such preparation for war. Not finding the president there, he did assure himself some mischief was intended. Pocahontas hid him for a time, and sent them who pursued him

INDIANS AT PRAYER WITH RATTLES
(THEODOR DE BRY, 1590)

the clean contrary way to seek him. But by her means and extraordinary bribes and much trouble, in three days' travel at length he
found us in the midst of these turmoils.

This unhappy news the president swore him to conceal from
the company. And so dissembling his sorrow with the best countenances he could, when the night approached went safely aboard
with all his soldiers, leaving Opechancanough at liberty, according
to his promise, the better to have Powhatan in his return [debt].

Now so extremely Powhatan had threatened the death of his
men if they did not by some means kill Captain Smith that the next

day they appointed all the country should come to trade unarmed, yet, unwilling to be treacherous but that they were constrained, hating fighting with him almost as ill as hanging, such fear they had of bad success. [*Barbour, calling this an "ill-told tale," explains that Powhatan commanded Opechancanough to ambush Smith, but the Pamunkey's fear of Smith caused them to fail.*]

The next morning the sun had not long appeared but the fields appeared covered with people and baskets to tempt us on shore. But nothing was to be had without his presence, nor they would not endure the sight of a gun. When the president saw them begin to depart, being unwilling to lose such a booty, he so well contrived the pinnace and his barges with ambushes as only with Lieutenant Percy, Master West, and Master Russell, with their arms went on shore. Others he appointed unarmed to receive what was brought.

The savages flocked before him in heaps, and the bank serving as a trench for a retreat, he drew them fair open to his ambushes. For he not being to be persuaded to go visit their king, the king knowing the most of them unarmed came to visit him with two or three hundred men, in the form of two half moons and with some twenty men and many women loaded with painted baskets. But when they approached somewhat near us, their women and children fled. For when they had environed and beset the fields in this manner, they thought their purpose sure, yet so trembled with fear as they were scarce able to nock their arrows. Smith standing with his three men ready bent, beholding them till they were within danger of our ambushes, who upon the word discovered themselves, and he retired to the barge. Which the savages no sooner perceived than away they fled, esteeming their heels for their best advantage.

That night we sent Master Crashaw and Master Ford to Jamestown to Captain Winne. In the way between Werowocomoco and the fort they met four or five of the Dutchmen's confederates going to

Powhatan, the which to excuse those gentlemen's suspicion of their running to the savages returned to the fort and there continued.

The savages hearing our barge go down the river in the night were so terribly afraid that we sent for more men (we having so much threatened their ruin and the razing of their houses, boats, and weirs) that the next day the king sent our captain a chain of pearl to alter his purpose and stay his men, promising though they wanted themselves to freight our ship and bring it aboard to avoid suspicion. So that five or six days after, from all parts of the country within ten or twelve miles in the extreme frost and snow, they brought us provision on their naked backs.

Yet notwithstanding this kindness and trade, had their art and poison been sufficient, the president, with Master West and some others, had been poisoned. It made them sick, but expelled itself. Wecuttanow, a stout young fellow, knowing he was suspected for bringing this present of poison with forty or fifty of his chief companions (seeing the president but with a few men at Potauncac) so proudly braved it, as though he expected to encounter a revenge. Which the president, perceiving in the midst of his company, did not only beat, but spurned him like a dog, as scorning to do him any worse mischief.

Whereupon all of them fled into the woods, thinking they had done a great matter to have so well escaped. And the townsmen remaining presently freighted our barge to be rid of our companies, framing many excuses to excuse Wecuttanow (being son to their chief king but Powhatan), and told us if we would show them him that brought the poison they would deliver him to us to punish as we pleased.

Men may think it strange there should be such a stir for a little corn, but had it been gold with more ease we might have got it; and had it wanted, the whole colony had starved. We may be thought very patient to endure all those injuries, yet only with fearing [*scaring*] them we got what they had. Whereas if we had taken revenge, then by their loss we should have lost ourselves.

We searched also the countries of Youghtanund and Mattapanient, where the people imparted that little they had with such complaints and tears from the eyes of women and children as he had been too cruel to have been a Christian that would not have been satisfied and moved with compassion, but had this happened in October, November, and December, when that unhappy discovery of Monacan was made and when we might have freighted a ship of forty tons, and twice as much might have been had from the rivers of Rappahannock, Patawomeck, and Pawtuxunt.

The main occasion of our thus temporizing with them was to part friends as we did, to give the less cause of suspicion to Powhatan to fly, by whom we now returned with a purpose to have surprised him and his provision. For effecting whereof (when we came against the town), the president sent Master Wiffin and Master Coe ashore to discover and make way for his intended project. But they found that those damned Dutchmen had caused Powhatan to abandon his new house and Werowocomoco, and to carry away all his corn and provision. And the people they found so ill affected that they were in great doubt how to escape with their lives.

So the president finding his intent frustrated, and that there was nothing now to be had and therefore an unfit time to revenge their abuses, sent Master Michael Phettiplace by land to Jamestown, whither we sailed with all the speed we could. We having in this journey (for 25 pounds of copper and 50 pounds of iron and beads) enough to keep 46 men six weeks, and every man for his reward a month's provision extraordinary (no trade being allowed but for the store), we got near 200 weight of deer suet and delivered to the cape merchant 479 bushels of corn.

Those temporizing proceedings to some may seem too charitable, to such a daily daring treacherous people, to others not pleasing that we washed not the ground with their bloods, nor showed such strange inventions in mangling, murdering, ransacking, and destroying (as did the Spaniards) the simple bodies of such ignorant souls; nor delightful, because not stuffed with relations of heaps and mines of gold and silver, nor such rare commodities as the Portuguese and Spaniards found in the East and West Indies. The want whereof hath begot us (that were the first undertakers) no less scorn and contempt than the noble conquests and valiant adventures beautified with it praise and honor. Too much, I confess, the world cannot attribute to their ever memorable merit. And to clear us from the blind world's ignorant censure, these few words may suffice any reasonable understanding.

It was the Spaniards' good hap to happen in those parts where were infinite numbers of people who had manured the ground with that providence it afforded victuals at all times. And time had brought them to that perfection [that] they had the use of gold and silver and the most of such commodities as those countries afforded. So that what the Spaniard got was chiefly the spoil and pillage of those country people, and not the labors of their own hands.

But had those fruitful countries been as savage, as barbarous, as ill peopled, as little planted, labored, and manured as Virginia, their proper labors it is likely would have produced as small profit as ours. But had Virginia been peopled, planted, manured, and adorned with such store of precious jewels and rich commodities as was the Indies then, had we not gotten and done as much as by their examples might be expected from us, the world might then have traduced us and our merits, and have made shame and infamy our recompense and reward.

But we chanced in a land even as God made it, where we found only an idle, improvident, scattered people, ignorant of the knowledge of gold or silver, or any commodities, and careless of anything but from hand to mouth, except baubles of no worth—nothing to encourage us but what accidentally we found nature afforded. Which ere we could bring to recompense our pains, defray our charges, and satisfy our adventurers, we were to discover [*explore*] the country, subdue the people, bring them to be tractable, civil, and industrious, and teach them trades that the fruits of their labors might make us some recompense, or plant such colonies of our own that must first make provision how to live of themselves ere they can bring to perfection the commodities of the country, which doubtless will be as commodious for England as the West Indies for Spain, if it be rightly managed, notwithstanding all our homebred opinions that will argue the contrary, as formerly some have done against the Spaniards and Portuguese.

But to conclude, against all rumor of opinion, I only say this. For those that the three first years began this plantation—notwithstanding all their factions, mutinies, and miseries, so gently corrected, and well prevented—peruse the Spanish decades, the relations of Master Hakluyt [*whose* Principal Navigations *was published in* 1589], and tell me how many ever with such small means as a barge of two tons, sometimes with seven, eight, or nine, or but at most twelve or sixteen men, did ever discover so many fair and navigable rivers, subject so many several kings, people, and nations to obedience and contribution, with so little bloodshed.

And if in the search of those countries we had happened where wealth had been, we had as surely had it as obedience and contribution. But if we have overskipped it, we will not envy them that shall find it, yet can we not but lament it was our fortunes to end when we had but only learned how to begin, and found the right course how to proceed.

CHAPTER SEVEN

The Coup against Smith

March to October 1609

BY THE SPRING OF 1609 *the colony was actually making some progress. The settlement was expanding, some 40 acres had been planted, and even manufacturing was progressing, with soap ash, pitch, tar, and glass works. The colonists were weaving Indian-style fishing weirs and nets, and they had dug a well that gave "excellent sweet water."*

But the colony lived constantly on the edge of disaster—with no room for error, a small problem could have enormous consequences. That summer it was rats. Stowaways on the English ships, the rats multiplied into the thousands and infested the casks of corn that the settlers expected to live on through the fall. Those who were thrifty managed, supplementing their meager diet with wild game and berries, but with the heat settling in, most people would rather trade what few valuables they had than do enough honest work to stay alive. Those who do not work, Smith ordered, will not eat. Smith promised to punish idlers and hang those who attempted an escape to Newfoundland (as some were plotting). Although many complained of his

harsh rule, it is also true that relatively few colonists died during his administration—only 18 out of 200, 11 of them by drowning when they were out
foraging, against Smith's orders.

Smith's answer to laziness and disobedience was military discipline.
He had his soldiers drill in a clearing outside the fort, blasting away at
trees. The bonus was the Indian audience, who watched in amazement
and great respect.

Smith still had to deal with the traitors who were building a house
for Powhatan. When one of them was heading back to Jamestown, Smith
went out to cut him off and ended up tangling with the king of the Paspahegh, a "strong stout savage." The Indian later escaped and Smith sent
Captain Peter Winne after him with 50 men. Winne only got himself into
a skirmish and riled up the Paspahegh. They would not back down until
Smith himself showed up, and then he and the Indians agreed to let the
matter rest so that peaceful trade could continue.

Among other events, a search by Sicklemore and others for Sir Walter
Raleigh's lost colonists was fruitless. And a Swiss named Volday was sent
out to bring his countrymen back from Powhatan's camp. Volday turned
traitor himself and became involved in a nebulous plot to help Powhatan
destroy Jamestown. But two laborers got word of the plot and informed
Smith. A delegation was sent to execute the traitors for treason. Powhatan
disavowed all knowledge of the plot. But before the execution could take
place, a scouting ship sailed up the James the week of July 9, commanded
by a mariner named Samuel Argall. He brought news that a third supply
of colonists would arrive later that summer. The hope of fresh provisions
brought some relief to the stressed colony.

In August 1609 the first of a fleet of nine ships loaded with 500 new
settlers, including women and children, arrived in Jamestown. One thing
was for sure, the Virginia Company was still serious about its Virginia colony. But it was also convinced that new management was in order—along
with a new governor named Thomas West, Lord De La Warr (older brother
of colonist Francis West). West had decided to come later; Sir Thomas Gates

would serve as governor until his arrival. John Smith's days in Virginia were drawing to a close.

The flagship of this new supply was lost during a bad storm, but the orders arrived with the first group in August. Thus began a lame-duck session for Smith, who refused to give up his power while Gates was still lost at sea. No one knew that Gates and company had miraculously survived by wrecking on Bermuda, and that they would finally limp into Jamestown the following May. Shakespeare would use accounts of the episode as inspiration for his last great play, The Tempest (circa 1611), in which the island (and by extension the Western Hemisphere) is a "brave new world."

In the meantime, young Francis West was chosen to be the new governor (same position as "president"), and even though Smith's one-year term was not up until September 10, the new administration proceeded almost as if he were already out. Smith, Ratcliffe, Scrivener, and six others were placed on the advisory council. Ratcliffe had newly returned from England, and it would not be long before he would regret it. The demotion naturally rankled Smith, who also scorned the new policy of trying to win the Indians over by introducing them to Christianity. But at least until his term expired he was still nominally in charge. In September he managed to get a weak successor elected, who immediately resigned; Smith then held on to his dictatorship for a few more weeks, until a coup dislodged him.

During that period he tried to keep the colony from starving by spreading it out. He sent one contingent down the James to Nansemond and another up to the falls, both with disastrous results. Neither group had the courage, experience, or smarts for dealing with the locals. Several of these tentative settlers were killed. John Martin, newly returned from England, proved particularly ineffectual. Smith himself took the barge and a few men up to the falls to assist in the establishment of the satellite fort near there. On the way up, he was surprised to see fort leader Francis West coming the other way. Nonetheless he went on and, finding the fort too near the river and in danger of flooding, tried to get the settlers to move closer to Powhatan village, even going so far as to try to buy the land from the Indians.

The settlers had already mistreated the Indians and did not want to move closer in, and they forced Smith away. But as he was leaving, a dozen Indians attacked the fort and killed a number of settlers. Those left swallowed their pride and begged Smith to return. Calling the attack a "poor silly assault," Smith with his usual bravado quickly ran the Indians off.

One night on the return trip, a spark ignited his gunpowder bag as he slept. Badly injured, he jumped overboard to put out the flames, and was pulled back in by his crew. Back at Jamestown, as Smith lay recovering, a complicated sequence of political intrigue resulted in a cabal of assassins apparently trying to kill him, but the would-be murderer lost heart. With only a few days left until Smith's term was over, George Percy was officially elected president instead of West. Smith decided it was time to go, that he would recover better in England. But Ratcliffe and a few others—who had tried to have Smith booted from the Council—were not content to just let him leave; they went around trying to collect written accounts of how he had abused his authority, including how he had supposedly plotted to marry Pocahontas and set up a kingdom for himself. The Virginia Company would dismiss the charges. Smith left Virginia in early October 1609, and never returned. Soon thereafter, the Dutch traitors got their just rewards.

WHEN THE SHIPS DEPARTED, all the provision of the store (but that the president had gotten) was so rotten with the last summer's rain, and eaten with rats and worms, as the hogs would scarcely eat it. Yet it was the soldiers' diet till our return, so that we found nothing done, but our victuals spent, and the most part of our tools and a good part of our arms conveyed to the savages.

But now casting up the store and finding sufficient till the next harvest, the fear of starving was abandoned, and the company divided into tens, fifteens, or as the business required. Six hours each day was spent in work, the rest in pastime and merry exercises, but the untowardness of the greatest number caused the president advise as followeth.

"Countrymen, the long experience of our late miseries I hope is sufficient to persuade everyone to a present correction of himself, And think not that either my pains nor the adventurers' purses will ever maintain you in idleness and sloth.

"I speak not this to you all, for divers of you I know deserve both honor and reward, better than is yet here to be had. But the greater part must be more industrious, or starve, however you have been heretofore tolerated by the authority of the Council, from that I have often commanded you. You see now that power resteth wholly in myself. You must obey this now for a law, that he that will not work shall not eat (except by sickness he be disabled). For the labors of thirty or forty honest and industrious men shall not be consumed to maintain a hundred and fifty idle loiterers.

"And though you presume the authority here is but a shadow—and that I dare not touch the lives of any but my own must answer it—the letters patents shall each week be read to you, whose contents will tell you the contrary. I would wish you therefore without contempt seek to observe these orders set down, for there are now no more councillors to protect you, nor curb my endeavors. Therefore he that offendeth, let him assuredly expect his due punishment." [*Smith was the final surviving member of the Council still in Virginia. Newport, Martin, and Ratcliffe had temporarily returned to England; Wingfield had left permanently; Gosnold and Kendall were dead. Of the new councillors, Scrivener and Waldo had recently died in the boating accident at Hog Island, and Peter Winne had just died without leaving evidence of the details.*]

He made also a table, as a public memorial of every man's deserts, to encourage the good and with shame to spur on the rest to amendment. By this many became very industrious, yet more by punishment performed their business, for all were so tasked that there was no excuse could prevail to deceive him. Yet the Dutchmen's consorts so closely conveyed them powder, shot, swords, and tools that, though we could find the defect, we could not find by whom, till it was too late.

All this time the Dutchmen remaining with Powhatan (who kindly entertained them to instruct the savages the use of our arms), and their consorts not following them as they expected, to know the cause they sent Francis their companion, a stout young fellow disguised like a savage to the glasshouse [*glassworks*], a place in the woods near a mile from Jamestown, where was their rendezvous for all their unsuspected villainy. Forty men they procured to lie in ambush for Captain Smith, who no sooner heard of this Dutchman but he sent to apprehend him (but he was gone) yet to cross his return to Powhatan.

The captain presently dispatched twenty shot after him, himself returning from the glasshouse alone. By the way he encountered the king of Paspahegh, a most strong stout savage, whose persuasions not being able to persuade him to his ambush, seeing him [*Smith*] only armed but with a falchion [*broad, curved sword*], attempted to have shot him. But the president prevented his shoot by grappling with him, and the savage as well prevented him for drawing his falchion, and perforce bore him into the river to have drowned him. Long they struggled in the water, till the president got such hold on his throat he had near strangled the king. But having drawn his falchion to cut off his head, seeing how pitifully he begged his life, he led him prisoner to Jamestown, and put him in chains.

The Dutchman ere long was also brought in, whose villainy though all this time it was suspected, yet he feigned such a formal excuse that for want of language Captain Winne understood him not rightly. [*Smith's story here is slightly out of sequence—Winne is still alive at this point but not for long.*] And for their dealings with Powhatan, [*the Dutchman said*] that to save their lives they were constrained to accommodate his arms, of whom he extremely complained to have detained them perforce, and that he made this escape with the

C: Smith takes the King of Paspahegh prisoner. A° 1609.

SMITH TAKES PASPAHEGH PRISONER
(ENGRAVING FROM 1624 *GENERAL HISTORY*).

hazard of his life, and meant not to have returned, but was only walking in the woods to gather walnuts.

Yet for all this fair tale, there was so small appearance of truth, and [*with*] the plain confession of Paspahegh of his treachery he went by the heels [*he was shackled*]. Smith purposing to regain the Dutchmen, by the saving his life, the poor savage did his best by his daily messengers to Powhatan. But all returned that the Dutchmen would not return, neither did Powhatan stay them, and to bring them fifty miles on his men's backs they were not able. Daily this king's wives, children, and people came to visit him with presents, which he liberally bestowed to make his peace. Much trust they had in the president's promise, but the king finding his guard negligent, though fettered yet escaped. Captain Winne, thinking to pursue him, found such troops of savages to hinder his passage as they exchanged many volleys of shot for flights of arrows.

Captain Smith hearing of this in returning to the fort took two savages prisoners, called Kemps and Tussore, the two most exact villains in all the country. With these he sent Captain Winne, and fifty choice men and Lieutenant Percy, to have regained the king and revenged this injury, and so had done if they had followed his directions, or been advised with those two villains that would have betrayed both king and kindred for a piece of copper. But he [Winne] trifling away the night, the savages the next morning by the rising of the sun braved him to come ashore to fight. A good time both sides let fly at other, but we heard of no hurt, only they took two canoes, burnt the king's house, and so returned to Jamestown.

The president fearing those bravados would but encourage the savages, began again himself to try his conclusions, whereby six or seven savages were slain, as many made prisoners. He burned their houses, took their boats with all their fishing weirs, and planted some of them at Jamestown for his own use, and now resolved not to cease till he had revenged himself of all them had injured him. But in his journey passing by Paspahegh toward Chickahamania, the savages did their best to draw him to their ambushes. But seeing him regardlessly pass their country, all showed themselves in their bravest manner. To try their valors he could not but let fly, and ere he could land, they no sooner knew him but they threw down their arms and desired peace.

Their orator was a lusty young fellow called Okaning, whose worthy discourse deserveth to be remembered. And thus it was:

"Captain Smith, my master is here present in the company, thinking it Captain Winne and not you. Of him [Winne] he intended to have been revenged, having never offended him. If he [king of Paspahegh] hath offended you in escaping your imprisonment, the fishes swim, the fowls fly, and the very beasts strive to escape the snare and live. Then blame not him being a man. He would entreat you remember, you being a prisoner what pains he took to save your life. If since he hath injured you, he was compelled to it. But howsoever, you have revenged it with our too great loss.

"We perceive and well know you intend to destroy us, that are here to entreat and desire your friendship, and to enjoy our houses and plant our fields, of whose fruit you shall participate. Otherwise you will have the worse by our absence, for we can plant anywhere, though with more labor, and we know you cannot live if you want our harvest and that relief we bring you. If you promise us peace, we will believe you; if you proceed in revenge we will abandon the country."

Upon these terms the president promised them peace till they did us injury, upon condition they should bring in provision. Thus all departed good friends, and so continued till Smith left the country.

Arriving at Jamestown, complaint was made to the president that the Chickahamanians, who all this while continued trade and seemed our friends by color thereof, were only thieves. And amongst other things a pistol being stolen and the thief fled, there was apprehended two proper young fellows that were brothers, known to be his confederates.

Now to regain this pistol, the one was imprisoned, the other was sent to return the pistol again within twelve hours, or his brother to be hanged. Yet the president pitying the poor naked savage in the dungeon, sent him victual and some charcoal for a fire. Ere midnight his brother returned with the pistol, but the poor savage in the dungeon was so smothered with the smoke he had made, and so piteously burned, that we found him dead. The other most lamentably bewailed his death, and broke forth into such bitter agonies, that the president to quiet him told him that if hereafter they would not steal, he would make him alive again. But he little thought he could be recovered. Yet we doing our best with aqua vitae and vinegar, it pleased God to restore him again to life, but so drunk and affrighted that he seemed lunatic—the which as much tormented and grieved the other as before to see him dead. Of which malady upon promise of their good behavior, the president promised to recover him, and so caused him to be laid by a fire to sleep, who in the morning having well slept had recovered his perfect senses. And then being dressed of his burning, and each a piece of copper given them, they went away so well contented that this was spread among all the savages for a miracle, that Captain Smith could make a man alive that was dead.

Another ingenuous savage of Powhatan's, having gotten a great bag of powder and the back of an armor [backpiece], at Werowocomoco amongst a many of his companions to show his extraordinary skill he did dry it on the back as he had seen the soldiers at Jamestown. But he dried it so long, they peeping over it to see his skill, it took fire and blew him to death, and one or two more, and the rest so scorched they had little pleasure to meddle any more with powder.

These and many other such pretty accidents so amazed and affrighted both Powhatan and all his people that from all parts with presents they desired peace, returning many stolen things which we never demanded nor thought of. And after that, those that were taken stealing both Powhatan and his people have sent them back to Jamestown to receive their punishment; and all the country became absolute as free for us as for themselves.

Now we so quietly followed our business that in three months we made three or four last [about 12 barrels per last] of tar, pitch, and soap ashes; produced a trial of glass; made a well in the fort of excellent sweet water, which till then was wanting; built some twenty houses; recovered our church; provided nets and weirs for fishing; and to stop the disorders of our disorderly thieves and the savages, built a blockhouse in the neck of our isle, kept by a garrison to entertain the savages' trade, and none to pass nor repass savage nor Christian without the president's order.

Thirty or forty acres of ground we digged and planted. Of three sows in eighteen months, increased sixty and odd pigs. And near 500 chickings brought up themselves without having any meat given them. But the hogs were transported to Hog Isle, where also we built a blockhouse with a garrison to give us notice of any shipping; and for their exercise they made clapboard and wainscot, and cut down trees. We built also a fort for a retreat near a convenient river upon a high commanding hill, very hard to be assaulted and easy to be defended, but ere it was finished this defect caused a stay:

In searching our casked corn, we found it half rotten and the rest so consumed with so many thousands of rats that increased so fast, but their original was from the ships [*the rats came from the ships*], as we knew not how to keep that little we had. This did drive us all to our wit's end, for there was nothing in the country but what nature afforded.

Until this time Kemps and Tassore were fettered prisoners, and did double task and taught us how to order and plant our fields, whom now for want of victual we set at liberty. But so well they liked our companies they did not desire to go from us. And to express their loves, for 16 days' continuance the country people brought us, when least, 100 a day of squirrels, turkeys, deer and other wild beasts.

But this want of corn occasioned the end of all our works, it being work sufficient to provide victual. Sixty or eighty with Ensign Laxon was sent down the river to live upon oysters, and twenty with Lieutenant Percy to try for fishing at Point Comfort. But in six weeks they would not agree once to cast out the net, he being sick and burned sore with gunpowder. Master West with as many went up to the falls, but nothing could be found but a few berries and acorns.

Of that in store every man had their equal proportion. Till this present, by the hazard and endeavors of some thirty or forty, this whole colony had ever been fed. We had more sturgeon than could be devoured by dog and man, of which the industrious by drying and pounding, mingled with caviar, sorrel, and other wholesome herbs would make bread and good meat. Others would gather as much *tockwhogh* [*tuckahoe*] roots in a day as would make them bread a week. So that of those wild fruits and what we caught, we lived very well in regard of such a diet. But such was the strange condition of some 150 that had they not been forced *nolens volens* [*willy-nilly*] perforce to gather and prepare their victual they would all have starved or have eaten one another.

Of those wild fruits the savages often brought us, and for that the president would not fulfill the unreasonable desire of those distracted gluttonous loiterers to sell not only our kettles, hoes, tools, and iron, nay swords, pieces, and the very ordnance and houses, might they have prevailed to have been but idle. For those savage fruits, they would have had imparted all to the savages, especially for one basket of corn they heard of to be at Powhatan's, fifty miles from our fort. Though he bought near half of it to satisfy their humors, yet to have had the other half they would have sold their souls, though not sufficient to have kept them a week.

Thousands were their exclamations, suggestions, and devices to force him to those base inventions to have made it an occasion to abandon the country. Want perforce constrained him [*Smith*] to endure their exclaiming follies, till he found out the author—one Dyer, a most crafty fellow and his ancient maligner, whom he worthily punished. And with the rest he argued the case in this manner.

"Fellow soldiers, I did little think any so false to report, or so many to be so simple to be persuaded that I either intend to starve you, or that Powhatan at this present hath corn for himself, much less for you; or that I would not have it, if I knew where it were to be had.

Neither did I think any so malicious as now I see a great many. Yet it shall not so passionate me, but I will do my best for my worst maligner. But dream no longer of this vain hope from Powhatan, nor that I will longer forbear to force you from your idleness and punish you if you rail. But if I find any more runners for Newfoundland with the pinnace, let him assuredly look to arrive at the gallows. You cannot deny but that by the hazard of my life many a time I have saved yours, when (might your own wills have prevailed) you would have starved. And will do still whether I will or no. But I protest by that God that made me, since necessity hath not power to force you to gather for yourselves those fruits the earth doth yield, you shall not only gather for yourselves but those that are sick. As yet I never had more from the store than the worst of you, and all my English extraordinary provision that I have you shall see me divide it amongst the sick. And this savage trash you so scornfully repine at, being put in your mouths your stomachs can digest. If you would have better you should have brought it, and therefore I will take a course you shall provide what is to be had. The sick shall not starve, but equally share of all our labors. And he that gathereth not every day as much as I do, the next day shall be set beyond the river and be banished from the fort as a drone, till he amend his conditions or starve."

This order many murmured was very cruel, but it caused the most part so well bestir themselves that of 200 (except they were drowned) there died not past seven. As for Captain Winne and Master Leigh, they were dead ere this want happened, and the rest died not for want of such as preserved the rest. Many were billeted amongst the savages, whereby we knew all their passages, fields, and habitations, how to gather and use their fruits as well as themselves. For they did know we had such a commanding power at Jamestown they dared not wrong us of a pin.

So well those poor savages used us that were thus billeted that divers of the soldiers ran away to search Kemps and Tassore our old prisoners. Glad were these savages to have such an opportunity to testify their love unto us. For instead of entertaining them [*the deserters*] and such things as they had stolen, with all their great offers and promises they made them how to revenge their injuries upon Captain Smith, Kemps first made himself sport in showing his countrymen (by them) how he was used, feeding them with this law: who would not work must not eat, till they were near starved indeed, continually threatening to beat them to death. Neither could they get from him, till he and his consorts brought them perforce to our captain that so well contented him and punished them, as many others that intended also to follow them were rather contented to labor at home than adventure to live idlely amongst the savages, of whom there was more hope to make better Christians and good subjects than the one half of those that counterfeited themselves both. [*The former prisoner Kemps refused to listen to the deserters, telling them instead that as at Jamestown so among the Indians—they must work for a living; he even brought them back to Jamestown for a reward.*]

For so afraid was all those kings and the better sort of the people to displease us that some of the baser sort that we have extremely hurt and punished for their villainies would hire us. We should not tell it to their kings or countrymen, who would also repunish them, and yet return them to Jamestown to content the president for a testimony of their loves.

Master Sicklemore well returned from Chawanoac, but found little hope and less certainty of them were left by Sir Walter Raleigh. The river he saw was not great, the people few, the country most overgrown with pines where there did grow here and there, stragglingly, *pemminaw*—we call silk grass. But by the river the ground was good and exceeding fertile.

Master Nathaniel Powell and Anas Todkill were also by the Quiyoughcohanocks conducted to the Mangoags to search them there, but nothing could they learn but they were all dead. This honest proper good promise-keeping king, of all the rest did ever best affect us. And though to his false gods he was very zealous, yet he would confess our god as much exceeded his as our guns did his bow and arrows, often sending our president many presents to pray to his god for rain or his corn would perish, for his gods were angry. Three days' journey they conducted them through the woods, into a high country toward the southwest, where they saw here and there a little cornfield by some little spring or small brook, but no river they could see. The people in all respects like the rest (except their language), they live most upon roots, fruits, and wild beasts, and trade with them toward the sea and the fatter countries for dried fish, and corn for skins.

All this time to recover the Dutchmen and one Bentley, another fugitive, we employed one William Volday, a Switzer by birth, with pardons and promises to regain them. Little we then suspected this double villain of any villainy; who plainly taught us in the most trust was the greatest treason. For this wicked hypocrite, by the seeming hate he bore to the lewd conditions of his cursed countrymen, having this opportunity by his employment to regain them, conveyed them everything they desired to effect their projects to destroy the colony. With much devotion they expected the Spaniard, to whom they intended good service, or any other that would but carry them from us.

But to begin with the first opportunity: They seeing necessity thus enforced us to disperse ourselves, importuned Powhatan to lend them but his forces and they would not only destroy our hogs, fire our town, and betray our pinnace, but bring to his service and subjection the most of our company. With this plot they had acquainted many discontents, and many were agreed to their devilish practice. But one Thomas Douse and Thomas Mallard (whose Christian hearts relented at such an unchristian act) voluntarily revealed it to Captain Smith, who caused them to conceal it, persuading Douse and Mallard to proceed in their confederacy, only to bring the irreclaimable Dutchmen and the inconstant savages in such a manner amongst such ambushes as he had prepared that not many of them should return from our peninsula.

But this bruit coming to the ears of the impatient multitude, they so importuned the president to cut off those Dutchmen as amongst many that offered to cut their throats before the face of Powhatan. The first was Lieutenant Percy, and Master John Cuderington, two gentlemen of as bold resolute spirits as could possibly be found. But the president had occasion of other employment for them, and gave way to Master Wiffin and Sergeant Jeffrey Abbot, to go and stab them or shoot them. But the Dutchmen made such excuses, accusing Volday whom they supposed had revealed their project, as Abbot would not yet Wiffin would—perceiving it but deceit.

The king understanding of this their employment sent presently his messengers to Captain Smith to signify it was not his fault to detain them, nor hinder his men from executing his command; nor did he nor would he maintain them or any to occasion his displeasure.

But whilst this business was in hand, arrived one Captain Argall and Master Thomas Sedan, sent by Master Cornelius to truck [trade] with the colony and fish for sturgeon, with a ship well furnished with wine and much other good provision. Though it was not sent us, our necessities was such as enforced us to take it.

He brought us news of a great supply and preparation for the Lord La Warr, with letters that much taxed our president for his hard dealing with the savages and not returning the shipper freighted. Notwithstanding, we kept this ship till the fleet arrived. True it is, Argall lost his voyage, but we revictualed him and sent him for England, with a true relation of the causes of our defailments and how impossible it was to return that wealth they expected or observe their instructions to endure the savages' insolences, or do anything to any purpose except they would send us men and means that could produce that they so much desired. Otherwise all they did was lost, and could not but come to confusion.

The villainy of Volday we still dissembled. Adam upon his pardon came home but Samuel still stayed with Powhatan to hear further of their estates by this supply.

Now all their plots Smith so well understood [that] they were his best advantages to secure us from any treachery could be done by them or the savages, which with facility he could revenge when he would because all those countries more feared him than Powhatan. And he had such parties with all his bordering neighbors. And many of the rest for love or fear would have done anything he would have them upon any commotion though these fugitives had done all they could to persuade Powhatan [that] King James would kill Smith for using him and his people so unkindly.

By this you may see for all those crosses, treacheries, and dissensions how he wrestled and overcame (without bloodshed) all that happened—also what good was done, how few died, what food the country naturally affordeth, what small cause there is men should starve or be murdered by the savages that have discretion to manage them with courage and industry.

The two first years, though by his adventures he had oft brought the savages to a tractable trade, yet you see how the envious authority ever crossed him and frustrated his best endeavors. But it wrought in him that experience and estimation amongst the savages as otherwise it had been impossible he had ever effected that [accomplished what] he did. Notwithstanding the many miserable yet generous [courageous] and worthy adventures he had oft and long endured in the wide world, yet in this case he was again to learn his lecture [lesson] by experience. Which with thus much ado having obtained, it was his ill chance to end when he had but only learned how to begin. And though he left those unknown difficulties (made easy and familiar) to his unlawful successors, who only by living in Jamestown presumed to know more than all the world could direct them, now though they had all his soldiers with a triple power and twice triple better means, by what they have done in his absence the world may see what they would have done in his presence had he not prevented their indiscretions. It doth justly prove what cause he had to send them for England, and that he was neither factious, mutinous, nor dishonest. But they have made it more plain since his return for England, having his absolute authority freely in their power, with all the advantages and opportunity that his labors had effected. As I am sorry their actions have made it so manifest, so I am unwilling to say what reason doth compel me, but only to make apparent the truth lest I should seem partial, reasonless, and malicious.

To redress those jars and ill proceedings, the treasurer, Council, and Company of Virginia, not finding that return and profit they expected and them engaged there, not having means to subsist of themselves, made means to his Majesty to call in their commission and take a new in their own names, as in their own publication, 1610 you may read at large.

Having thus annihilated the old by virtue of a commission made to the right honorable Sir Thomas West, Lord de la Warr, to be General of Virginia, Sir Thomas Gates his lieutenant, Sir George Somers admiral, Sir Thomas Dale high marshal, Sir Ferdinando Wainman general of the horse, and so all other offices to many other worthy gentlemen for their lives (though not any of them had ever been in Virginia, except Captain Newport, who was also by patent made vice admiral) those noble gentlemen drew in such great sums of money that they sent Sir Thomas Gates, Sir George Somers, and Captain Newport with nine ships and five hundred people, who had each of them a commission who first arrived to call in the old without the knowledge or consent of them that had endured all those former dangers to beat the path—not any regard had at all of them.

All things being ready, because those three captains could not agree for place, it was concluded they should go all in one ship. So all their three commissions were in that ship with them called the *Sea Venture*.

They set sail from England in May 1609. A small ketch perished at sea in a hurricane. The admiral with a hundred and fifty men with the two knights and their new commission, their bills of loading with all manner of directions, and the most part of their provision arrived not.

With the other seven ships as captains arrived Ratcliffe (whose right name, as is said, was Sicklemore), Martin and Archer with Captain Wood, Captain Webbe, Captain Moone, Captain King, Captain Davis, and divers gentlemen of good means and great parentage. But the first, as they had been troublesome at sea, began again to mar all ashore. For though (as is said) they were formerly sent for England, yet now returning again graced by the titles of captains of the passengers, seeing the admiral wanting and great probability of her loss, strengthened themselves with those new companies, so exclaiming against Captain Smith that they mortally hated him ere ever they saw him.

Who [Smith] understanding by his scouts the arrival of such a fleet, little dreaming of any such supply, supposed them Spaniards. But he quickly so determined and ordered our affairs as we little feared their arrival, nor the success of our encounter. Nor were the savages any way negligent for the most part to aid and assist us with their best power.

Had it so been, we had been happy, for we would not have trusted them but as our foes. Where receiving them as our countrymen and friends, they did what they could to murder our president, to surprise the store, the fort, and our lodgings, to usurp the government, and make us all their servants and slaves, till they could consume us and our remembrance, and rather indeed to supplant us than supply us, as Master William Box an honest gentleman in this voyage thus relateth:

"In the tail of a hurricane, we were separated from the admiral, which although it was but the remainder of that storm there is seldom any such in England or those northern parts of Europe. Some lost their masts, some their sails blown from their yards, the seas so over-raking our ships much of our provision was spoiled, our fleet separated, and our men sick. And many died. And in this miserable estate we arrived in Virginia."

To a thousand mischiefs those lewd captains led this lewd company, wherein were many unruly gallants packed thither by their friends to escape ill destinies. And those would dispose and determine of the government—sometimes to one, the next day to another. Today the old commission must rule, tomorrow the new, the next day neither. In fine, they would rule all or ruin all. Yet in charity we must endure them thus to destroy us, or by correcting their follies have brought the world's censure upon us to be guilty of their bloods. Happy had we been had they never arrived and we forever abandoned and, as we were, left to our fortunes. For on earth for the number was never more confusion or misery than their factions occasioned.

The president seeing the desire those braves had to rule, seeing how his authority was so unexpectedly changed, would willingly have left all and have returned for England. But seeing there was small hope this new commission would arrive, longer he would not suffer those factious spirits to proceed. It would be too tedious, too strange, and almost incredible should I particularly relate the infinite dangers, plots, and practices he daily escaped amongst this factious crew, the chief whereof he quickly laid by the heels till his leisure better served to do them justice.

And to take away all occasions of further mischief, Master Percy had his request granted to return for England, being very sick. And Master West with a hundred and twenty of the best he could choose, he sent to the falls, Martin with near as many to Nansemond with their due proportions of all provisions according to their numbers.

Now the president's year being near expired, he made Captain Martin president to follow the order for the election of a president every year. But he, knowing his own insufficiency and the company's untowardness and little regard of him, within three hours after resigned it again to Captain Smith, and at Nansemond thus proceeded.

The people [of Nansemond] being contributors used him kindly; yet such was his jealous fear [that] in the midst of their mirth he did surprise this poor naked king, with his monuments, houses, and the isle he inhabited, and there fortified himself, but so apparently distracted with fear as emboldened the savages to assault him, kill his men, release their king, gather and carry away a thousand bushels of corn, he not once offering to intercept them; but sent to the president then at the falls for thirty good shot, which from Jamestown immediately was sent him. But he so well employed them they did just nothing, but returned complaining of his tenderness. Yet he came away with them to Jamestown, leaving his company to their fortunes.

Here I cannot omit the courage of George Forest, that had seventeen arrows sticking in him and one shot through him, yet lived six or seven days as if he had small hurt, then for want of surgery died.

Master West having seated his men by the falls presently returned to revisit Jamestown. The president followed him to see that company seated, met him by the way, wondering at his so quick return, and found his company planted so inconsiderately in a place not only subject to the river's inundation but round environed with many intolerable inconveniences.

MAJOR POWHATAN VILLAGES AND ENGLISH
SETTLEMENTS AND FORTS, 1607-11

For remedy whereof he presently sent to Powhatan to sell him the place called Powhatan, promising to defend him against the Monacans. And these should be his conditions (with his people)—to resign him the fort and houses and all that country for a proportion of copper; that all stealing offenders should be sent him there to receive their punishment; that every house as a custom should pay him a bushel of corn for an inch square of copper, and a proportion of *pocones*, as a yearly tribute to King James for their protection as a duty; what else they could spare to barter at their best discretions.

But both this excellent place and those good conditions did those furies refuse, condemning both him, his kind care and authority. So much they depended on the Lord General's new commission as they regarded none. The worst they could do to show their spites they did, supposing all the Monacan's country gold. And none should come there but whom they pleased.

I do more than wonder to think how only with five men he [Smith] either dared or would adventure as he did (knowing how greedy they were of his blood) to land amongst them and commit to imprisonment all the chieftains of those mutinies, till by their multitudes being a hundred and twenty they forced him to retire. Yet in that interim he surprised one of their boats, wherewith he returned to their ship where indeed was their provision, which also he took. And well it chanced he found the mariners so tractable and constant, or there had been small possibility he had ever escaped.

There were divers other of better reason and experience that from their first landing, hearing the general good report of his old soldiers and seeing with their eyes his actions so well managed with discretion—as Captain Wood, Captain Webbe, Captain Moone, Captain FitzJames, Master William Powell, Master Partridge, Master White, and divers others—when they perceived the malice of Ratcliffe and Archer and their faction, left their companies and ever rested his faithful friends. But the worst was that the poor savages that daily brought in their contribution to the president that disorderly company so tormented those poor souls by stealing their corn, robbing their gardens, beating them, breaking their houses, and keeping some prisoners that they daily complained to Captain Smith [that] he had brought them for protectors, worse enemies than the Monacans themselves. Which, though till then for his love they had endured, they desired pardon if hereafter they defended themselves, since he would not correct them [the newcomers] as they had long expected he would. So much they importuned him to punish their misdemeanors as they offered (if he would lead them) to fight for him against them.

But having spent nine days in seeking to reclaim them, showing them how much they did abuse themselves with these great gilded hopes of the South Sea mines, commodities, or victories they so madly conceived, then seeing nothing would prevail he set sail for Jamestown.

Now no sooner was the ship under sail but the savages assaulted those hundred and twenty in their fort, finding some straggling abroad in the woods. They slew many, and so affrighted the rest as their prisoners escaped. And they safely retired with the swords and cloaks of those they had slain. But ere we had sailed half a league, our ship grounding gave us once more liberty to summon them to a parley, where we found them all so strangely amazed with this poor silly assault of twelve savages that they submitted themselves upon any terms to the president's mercy; who presently put by the heels six or seven of the chief offenders.

The rest he seated gallantly at Powhatan in that savage fort, ready built and prettily fortified with poles and barks of trees, sufficient to have defended them from all the savages in Virginia—dry houses for lodgings and near two hundred acres of ground ready to be planted. And no place we knew so strong, so pleasant, and delightful in Virginia, for which we called it Nonesuch. The savages also he presently appeased, redelivering to either party their former losses. Thus all were friends.

New officers appointed to command and the president again ready to depart, at that instant arrived Captain West, whose gentle nature by the persuasions and compassion of those mutinous prisoners, alleging they had only done this for his honor, was so much abused that to regain their old hopes, new troubles did arise. For they ashore being possessed of all their victual, munition, and everything grew to that height in their former factions as the president left them to their fortunes. They returned again to the open air at West's Fort, abandoning Nonesuch, and he to Jamestown with his best expedition.

But this happened him in that journey.

Sleeping in his boat—for the ship was returned two days before—accidentally, one fired his powder bag, which tore the flesh

from his body and thighs, nine or ten inches square in a most pitiful manner. But to quench the tormenting fire, frying him in his
clothes, he leaped overboard into the deep river, where ere they
could recover him he was near drowned.

In this estate without either surgeon or surgery he was to go near
a hundred miles. Arriving at Jamestown, causing all things to be
prepared for peace or wars to obtain provision, whilst those things
were providing, Ratcliffe, Archer, and the rest of their confederates,
being to come to their trials [tests], their guilty consciences, fearing
a just reward for their deserts, seeing the president unable to stand
and near bereft of his senses by reason of his torment, they had
plotted to have murdered him in his bed. But his heart did fail him
that should have given fire to that merciless pistol. So not finding
that course to be the best, they joined together to usurp the government, thereby to escape their punishment.

The president had notice of their projects, the which to with-
stand, though his old soldiers importuned him but permit them
to take their heads that would resist his command, yet he would
not suffer them, but sent for the masters of the ships, and took order with them for his return for England. Seeing there was neither
surgeon nor surgery in the fort to cure his hurt and the ships to
depart the next day, his commission to be suppressed he knew not
why, himself and soldiers to be rewarded he knew not how, and a
new commission granted they knew not to whom (the which disabled that authority he had, as made them presume so oft to those
mutinies as they did)—besides, so grievous were his wounds and so
cruel his torments (few expecting he could live), nor was he able
to follow his business to regain what they had lost, suppress those
factions, and range the countries for provision as he intended—and
well he knew in those affairs his own actions and presence was as
requisite as his directions, which now could not be, he went presently abroad, resolving there to appoint them governors and to

take order [*measures*] for the mutineers. But he could find none he thought fit for it would accept it.

In the meantime, seeing him gone they persuaded Master Percy to stay, who was then to go for England, and be their president. Within less than an hour was this mutation begun and concluded. For when the company understood Smith would leave them, and saw the rest in arms called presidents and councillors, divers began to fawn on those new commanders that now bent all their wits to get him resign them his commission, who after much ado and many bitter repulses that their confusion (which he told them was at their elbows) should not be attributed to him for leaving the colony without a commission, he was not unwilling they should steal it. But never would he give it to such as they.

But had that unhappy blast not happened, he would quickly have qualified the heat of those humors and factions had the ships but once left them and us to our fortunes and have made that provision from among the savages, as we neither feared Spaniard, savage, nor famine; nor would have left Virginia, nor our lawful authority, but at as dear a price as we had bought it and paid for it. What shall I say but thus: We left him that in all his proceedings made justice his first guide and experience his second, even hating baseness, sloth, pride, and indignity more than any dangers; that never allowed more for himself than his soldiers with him; that upon no danger would send them where he would not lead them himself; that would never see us want what he either had, or could by any means get us; that would rather want than borrow, or starve than not pay; that loved action more than words and hated falsehood and covetousness worse than death; whose adventures were our lives, and whose loss our deaths.

Leaving us thus with three ships, seven boats, commodities ready to trade, the harvest newly gathered, ten weeks' provision in the store, four hundred ninety and odd persons, twenty-four pieces of ordnance, three hundred muskets, snaphances [*spring-lock muskets*] and firelocks, shot, powder, and match sufficient, cuirasses [*breastplates*], pikes, swords, and morions [*helmets*] more than men; the savages, their language and habitations well known to a hundred well trained and expert soldiers; nets for fishing; tools of all sorts to work; apparel to supply our wants; six mares and a horse; five or six hundred swine; as many hens and chickens; some goats; some sheep; what was brought or bred there remained. But they regarding nothing but from hand to mouth did consume that we had, took care for nothing but to perfect some colorable complaints against Captain Smith. For effecting whereof three weeks longer they stayed the ships, till they could produce them. That time and charge might much better have been spent, but it suited well with the rest of their discretions.

Now all those Smith had either whipped, punished, or any way disgraced, had free power and liberty to say or swear anything, and from a whole armful of their examinations this was concluded.

The mutineers at the falls complained he caused the savages assault them, for that he would not revenge their loss they being but 120, and he five men and himself. And this they proved by the oath of one he had oft whipped for perjury and pilfering. The Dutchmen that he had appointed to be stabbed for their treacheries swore he sent to poison them with ratsbane; the prudent Council, that he would not submit himself to their stolen authority; Coe and Dyer, that should have murdered him, were highly preferred for swearing. They heard one say he heard Powhatan say that he heard a man say: If the king would not send that corn he had, he should not long enjoy his copper crown, nor those robes he had sent him. Yet those also swore he might have had corn for tools but would not. The truth was Smith had no such engines as the king demanded, nor Powhatan any corn. Yet this [*faction*] argued he would starve them.

Other complained he would not let them rest in the fort (to starve) but forced them to the oyster banks to live or starve, as he lived himself. For though he had of his own private provisions sent from England sufficient, yet he gave it all away to the weak and sick, causing the most untoward (by doing as he did) to gather their food from the unknown parts of the rivers and woods, that they lived (though hardly) that otherwise would have starved ere they would have left their beds or, at most, the sight of Jamestown to have got their own victual.

Some prophetical spirit calculated he had the savages in such subjection he would have made himself a king by marrying Pocahontas, Powhatan's daughter. It is true she was the very nonpareil of his kingdom, and at most not past 13 or 14 years of age. Very oft she came to our fort with what she could get for Captain Smith that ever loved and used all the country well. But her especially he ever much respected, and she so well requited it that when her father intended to have surprised him she by stealth in the dark night came through the wild woods and told him of it. But her marriage could no way have entitled him by any right to the kingdom, nor was it ever suspected he had ever such a thought or more regarded her, or any of them, than in honest reason and discretion he might. If he would he might have married her, or have done what him listed. For there was none that could have hindered his determination.

Some that knew not anything to say, the Council instructed and advised what to swear. So diligent they were in this business that what any could remember he had ever done or said in mirth or passion, by some circumstantial oath, it was applied to their fittest use. Yet not past eight or nine could say much and that nothing but circumstances, which all men did know was most false and untrue. Many got their passes by promising in England to say much against him.

I have presumed to say this much in his behalf for that I never heard such foul slanders, so certainly believed and urged for truths by many a hundred that do still not spare to spread them, say them, and swear them, that I think do scarce know him though they met him. Nor have they either cause or reason but their wills or zeal to rumor or opinion. For the honorable and better sort of our Virginian adventurers, I think they understand it as I have writ it. For instead of accusing him, I have never heard any give him a better report than many of those witnesses themselves that were sent only home to testify against him.

Besides Jamestown that was strongly palisaded, containing some fifty or sixty houses, he left five or six other several forts and plantations. Though they were not so sumptuous as our successors expected, they were better than they provided any for us.

All this time we had but one carpenter in the country and three others that could do little, but desired to be learners: two blacksmiths, two sailors, and those we write "laborers" were for most part footmen and such as they that were adventurers brought to attend them, or such as they could persuade to go with them that never did know what a day's work was, except the Dutchmen and Poles and some dozen other. For all the rest were poor gentlemen, tradesmen, serving-men, libertines, and suchlike, ten times more fit to spoil a commonwealth than either begin one or but help to maintain one. For when neither the fear of God, nor the law, nor shame, nor displeasure of their friends could rule them here, there is small hope ever to bring one in twenty of them ever to be good there. Notwithstanding, I confess divers amongst them had better minds and grew much more industrious than was expected, yet ten good workmen would have done more substantial work in a day than ten of them in a week. Therefore men may rather wonder how we could do so much than use us so badly because we did no more but leave those examples to make others beware, and the fruits of all, we know not for whom.

But to see the justice of God upon these Dutchmen! Volday, before spoke of, made a shift to get for England, where persuading the merchants what rich mines he had found and great service he would do them was very well rewarded, and returned with the Lord La Warr. But being found a mere imposter, he died most miserably. Adam and Francis, his two consorts, were fled again to Powhatan to whom they promised at the arrival of my lord what wonders they would do would he suffer them but to go to him. But the king seeing they would be gone replied, "You that would have betrayed Captain Smith to me will certainly betray me to this great lord for your peace." So caused his men to beat out their brains.

CHAPTER EIGHT

Jamestown without Smith

October 1609 to 1611

ALMOST IMMEDIATELY AFTER *Smith's departure, things went down-hill for the colony. Powhatan no longer had any fear of the English, but he did have plenty of built-up resentment. A group of 17 colonists went to Kecoughtan to barter for supplies; they disappeared without a trace. The bodies of other white men were found a few days later, with bread stuffed in their mouths. Ratcliffe went to Powhatan to try to get food; he clearly had learned nothing from Smith. Of the 50 men he took, only 17 returned. His own death was among the worst.*

Then the real atrocities began. One party managed to squeeze a boatload of corn from some Indians, but had to decapitate two in the process—fright-ened, they sailed for England, leaving the colony to deal with the fallout. The colonists began to starve, and they ate every animal they could find; then they started in on shoe leather. One man killed and ate his pregnant wife, for which he was burned. Others wandered helplessly in the woods looking for food, only to be killed by Indian marauders who could practically

ARRIVAL OF LORD DE LA WARR IN JAMESTOWN
(19TH-CENTURY ENGRAVING)

smell the weakened animal that was the colony. Of the 500 colonists alive when Smith left, only 60 were living six months later.

In May 1610 Gates and the flagship arrived from Bermuda. Stunned by the condition of the colony, and realizing it only had enough food to last 16 days, he ordered Jamestown abandoned. The survivors loaded onto the four small ships, Gates boarding last to prevent anyone from burning the village in resentment. That would have been the end, except for the arrival of Baron de la Warr who, with 300 passengers and a year's worth of supplies, intercepted the escaping colonists in the James. De La Warr, who soon became governor, seemed to be the capable leader that Jamestown needed. But he became ill shortly after he arrived and left within the year.

In its first four years, then, the colony prospered only under Smith. During his time, political stability, economic vitality, and peace with the

Indians, though limited and based on autocratic rule, kept the beachhead from going under. But to make this colony stick and grow, the company had to keep sending fresh administrators and settlers and hope that some new combination would work. One thing working in Virginia's favor was that, because of its incompetence, Spain did not bother to attack it.

The next excerpt from Smith presents a summary of his time in Virginia. Following this are his reasons for conquering uncivilized lands. Notice that his statement "we are much alike at the hour of our birth," which has been cited as proof of his egalitarian vision, is really intended as a spur toward greater empire—in his time an honor to God and king.

THE DAY BEFORE CAPTAIN SMITH returned for England with the ships, Captain Davis arrived in a small pinnace with some sixteen proper men more. To these were added a company from Jamestown, under the command of Captain John Sicklemore, alias Ratcliffe, to inhabit Point Comfort. Captain Martin and Captain West, having lost their boats and near half their men among the savages, were returned to Jamestown. For the savages no sooner understood Smith was gone, but they all revolted and did spoil and murder all they encountered.

Now we were all constrained to live only on that Smith had only for his own company. For the rest had consumed their proportions, and now they had twenty presidents with all their appurtenances. Master Percy, our new president, was so sick he could neither go nor stand. But ere all was consumed, Captain West and Captain Sicklemore, each with a small ship and thirty or forty men well appointed, sought abroad to trade.

Sicklemore, upon the confidence of Powhatan, with about thirty others as careless as himself were all slain. Only Jeffrey Shortridge escaped, and Pocahontas the king's daughter saved a boy called Henry Spelman that lived many years after, by her means, amongst the Patawomecks. [Percy reported that Ratcliffe (Sicklemore) was captured *alive, then* "*bound unto a tree naked with a fire before, and by women his flesh was scraped from his bones with mussel shells and, before his face, thrown in the fire; and so for want of circumspection miserably perished.*"]

Powhatan still as he found means cut off their boats, denied them trade, so that Captain West set sail for England. Now we all found the loss of Captain Smith. Yea, his greatest maligners could now curse his loss. As for corn, provision, and contribution [tribute] from the savages, we had nothing but mortal wounds with clubs and arrows. As for our hogs, hens, goats, sheep, horse, or what lived, our commanders, officers, and savages daily consumed them. Some small proportions sometimes we tasted, till all was devoured. Then swords, arms, pieces, or anything, we traded with the savages, whose cruel fingers were so oft imbrued in our bloods that what by their cruelty, our governors' indiscretion, and the loss of our ships, of five hundred [colonists] within six months after Captain Smith's departure there remained not past sixty men, women, and children—most miserable and poor creatures. And those were preserved for the most part by roots, herbs, acorns, walnuts, berries, now and then a little fish. They that had starch in these extremities made no small use of it. Yea, even the very skins of our horses. Nay, so great was our famine that a savage we slew and buried; the poorer sort took him up again and ate him, and so did divers one another, boiled and stewed with roots and herbs. And one amongst the rest did kill his wife, powdered [salted] her, and had eaten part of her before it was known, for which he was executed, as he well deserved. Now whether she was better roasted, boiled, or carbonadoed [grilled] I know not, but of such a dish as powdered wife I never heard of.

This was that time which still to this day we called the starving time. It were too vile to say and scarce to be believed what we endured. But the occasion [cause] was our own—for want of providence, industry and government—and not the barrenness and defect of the

JAMESTOWN COLONISTS ON MEAGER RATIONS IN POST-SMITH
"STARVING TIME" (19TH-CENTURY ENGRAVING)

country, as is generally supposed. For till then in three years, for the numbers [of colonists] were landed us, we had never from England provision sufficient for six months, though it seemed by the bills of loading sufficient was sent us. Such a glutton is the sea (and such "good fellows" the mariners), we as little tasted of the great proportion sent us as they of our want and miseries. Yet, notwithstanding, they ever over-swayed and ruled the business, though we endured all that is said and chiefly lived on what this good country naturally afforded. Yet had we been even in paradise itself with these governors, it would not have been much better with us. Yet there was amongst us who had they had the government as Captain Smith appointed (but that they could not maintain it) would surely have kept us from those extremities of miseries. This in ten days more would have supplanted us all with death.

But God that would not this country should be unplanted sent Sir Thomas Gates and Sir George Somers with one hundred and fifty people, most happily preserved by the Bermudas, to preserve us. Strange it is to say how miraculously they were preserved in a leaking ship, as at large you may read in the ensuing history of those islands. [Smith relates the Bermuda episode in the fifth book of his General History. From the wreckage of the Sea Venture, commander Somers supervised the building of two pinnaces, while his 150 passengers survived on the island's plentiful fruit and wild hogs. After nine months on the island—during which a splinter group tried to mutiny so they could stay on Bermuda—the colonists finally were able to sail away, arriving in Jamestown on May 22, 1610. In June, Somers returned to Bermuda to gather hogs for the colony. He died there five months later of overwork and overeating. The Virginia Company renamed the island cluster the Summer Islands for its climate and for one of history's great mariners.]

When these two noble knights did see our miseries, being but strangers in that country and could understand no more of the cause but by conjecture of our clamors and complaints of accusing and excusing one another, they embarked us with themselves with the best means they could and abandoning Jamestown set sail for England. Whereby you may see the event of the government of the former commanders left to themselves, although they had lived there many years as formerly hath been spoken, who hindered now their proceedings, Captain Smith being gone.

At noon they fell to the Isle of Hogs, and the next morning to Mulberry Point, at what time they descried the longboat of the Lord La Warr, for God would not have it [Jamestown] so abandoned. For this honorable lord, then governor of the country, met them with three ships exceedingly well furnished with all necessaries fitting, who again returned them to the abandoned Jamestown. [Lord De La Warr arrived in June 1610, but he fell sick of dysentery and scurvy and had to return to England some nine months later.]

A brief relation written by Captain Smith to his Majesty's commissioners for the reformation of Virginia, concerning some aspersions against it:

Being enjoined by our commission not to unplant nor wrong the savages, because the channel was so near the shore where now is Jamestown (then a thick grove of trees), we cut them down where the savages—pretending as much kindness as could be—they hurt and slew one and twenty [a boy killed and 16-18 others injured] of us in two hours. At this time our diet was for most part water and bran, and three ounces of little better stuff in bread for five men a meal. And thus we lived near three months, our lodgings under boughs of trees, the savages being our enemies, whom we neither knew nor understood—occasions I think sufficient to make men sick and die.

Necessity thus did enforce me with eight or nine to try conclusions amongst the savages, [such] that we got provision which recovered the rest being most sick. Six weeks [three to four weeks] I was led captive by those barbarians. Though some of my men were slain and the rest fled, yet it pleased God to make their great king's daughter the means to return me safe to Jamestown and relieve our wants. And then our commonwealth was in all eight and thirty, the remainder of one hundred and five.

Being supplied with one hundred and twenty, with twelve men in a boat of three tons I spent fourteen weeks in those large waters. The contents of the way of my boat [*total length of the route*] protracted by the scale of proportion, was about three thousand miles [*more like 2,000-2,500*], besides the river we dwell upon, where no Christian known ever was, and our diet for the most part what we could find; yet but one died.

The savages being acquainted that by command from England we dared not hurt them, were much emboldened. That famine and their insolences did force me to break our commission and instructions, cause Powhatan fly his country, and take the king of Pamunkey prisoner; and also to keep the king of Paspahegh in shackles and put his men to double tasks in chains, till nine and thirty of their kings paid us contribution [*Smith exaggerates—not all paid tribute*] and the offending savages sent to Jamestown to punish at our own discretions. In the two last years I stayed there, I had not a man slain.

All those conclusions being not able to prevent the bad events of pride and idleness, having received another supply of seventy, we were about two hundred in all, but not twenty workmen. In following the strict directions from England to do that was impossible at that time, so it happened that neither we nor they had anything to eat but what the country afforded naturally. Yet of eighty who lived upon oysters in June and July, with a pint of corn a week for a man lying under trees, and 120 for the most part living upon sturgeon (which was dried till we pounded it to powder for meal), yet in ten weeks but seven died.

It is true, we had of tools, arms, and munition sufficient, some aqua vitae, vinegar, meal, peas, and oatmeal, but in two years and a half not sufficient for six months, though by the bills of loading the proportions sent us would well have contented us. Notwithstanding, we sent home ample proofs of pitch, tar, soap ashes, wainscot, clapboard, silk grass, iron ore, some sturgeon, and glass, sassafras, cedar, cyprus, and black walnut; crowned Powhatan, sought the Monacan's country, according to the instructions sent us. But they caused us neglect more necessary works. They had better have given for pitch and soap ashes one hundred pound a ton in Denmark. We also maintained five or six several plantations.

Jamestown being burned, we rebuilt it and three forts more. Besides the church and storehouse, we had about forty or fifty several houses to keep us warm and dry, environed with a palisade of fourteen or fifteen foot, and each as much as three or four men could carry. We dug a fair well of fresh water in the fort, where we had three bulwarks, four and twenty piece of ordnance—of culverin, demiculverin, sakre, and falcon—and most well mounted upon convenient platforms, planted one hundred acres of corn. We had but six ships to transport and supply us, and but two hundred seventy-seven men, boys, and women, by whose labors Virginia being brought to this kind of perfection, the most difficulties past, and the foundation thus laid by this small means. Yet because we had done no more, they called in our commission, took a new in their own names, and appointed us near as many offices and officers as I had soldiers, that neither knew us nor we them, without our consents or knowledge. Since, there have gone more than one hundred ships of other proportions, and eight or ten thousand people. [From 1606 to 1622 about 6,000 settlers were sent. The population in 1625 was 1,300; the others had left or died.]

Now if you please to compare what hath been spent, sent, discovered and done this fifteen years, by that we did in the three first years, and every governor that hath been there since, give you but such an account as this, you may easily find what hath been the cause of those disasters in Virginia.

Then came in Captain Argall and Master Sedan, in a ship of Master Cornelius, to fish for sturgeon, who had such good provision we contracted with them for it, whereby we were better furnished than ever.

Not long after came in seven ships, with about three hundred people, but rather to supplant us than supply us, their admiral with their authority being castaway in the Bermudas. Very angry they were we had made no better provision for them. Seven or eight weeks we withstood the inundations of these disorderly humors, till I was near blown to death with gunpowder, which occasioned me to return for England.

In the year 1609 about Michaelmas, I left the country, as is formerly related, with three ships, seven boats, commodities to trade, harvest newly gathered, eight weeks' provision of corn and meal, about five hundred persons, three hundred muskets, shot, powder, and match, with arms for more men than we had. The savages, their language, and habitation well known to two hundred expert soldiers; nets for fishing, tools of all sorts, apparel to supply their wants; six mares and a horse, five or six hundred swine, many more poultry, what was brought or bred, but victual there remained.

Having spent some five years, and more than five hundred pounds in procuring the letters patents and setting forward, and near as much more about New England, etc. Thus these nineteen years [1605-24] I have here and there not spared anything according to my ability, nor the best advice I could to persuade how those strange miracles of misery might have been prevented, which lamentable experience plainly taught me of necessity must ensue. But few would believe me, till now too dearly they have paid for it. Wherefore hitherto I have rather left all than undertake impossibilities, or anymore such costly tasks at such chargeable rates. For in neither of those two countries have I one foot of land, nor the very house I builded, nor the ground I digged with my own hands, nor ever any content or satisfaction at all. And though I see ordinarily those two countries shared before me by them that neither have them nor knows them but by my descriptions, yet that doth not so much trouble me as to hear and see those contentions and divisions which will hazard if not ruin the prosperity of Virginia, if present remedy be not found, as they have hindered many hundreds who would have been there ere now, and makes them yet that are willing to stand in a demur.

Our right to those countries, true reasons for plantations, rare examples:

Many good religious devout men have made it a great question, as a matter in conscience, by what warrant they might go to possess those countries which are none of theirs, but the poor savages'? Which poor curiosity will answer itself, for God did make the world to be inhabited with mankind, and to have his name known to all nations and from generation to generation.

As the people increased they dispersed themselves into such countries as they found most convenient. And here in Florida, Virginia, New England, and Canada is more land than all the people in Christendom can manure, and yet more to spare than all the natives of those countries can use and cultivate. And shall we here keep such a coil [turmoil] for land, and at such great rents and rates, when there is so much of the world uninhabited—and as much more in other places—and as good or rather better than any we possess, were it manured and used accordingly? If this be not a reason sufficient to such tender consciences, for a copper kettle and a few toys as beads and hatchets they will sell you a whole country; and for a small matter their houses and the ground they dwell upon; but those of the Massachusetts have resigned theirs freely.

Now the reasons for plantations are many. Adam and Eve did first begin this innocent work to plant the earth to remain to posterity, but not without labor, trouble, and industry. Noah and his family began again the second plantation, and their seed as it still increased hath still planted new countries, and one country another, and so the world to that estate it is, but not without much hazard, travel, mortalities, discontents, and many disasters. Had those worthy fathers and their memorable offspring not been more diligent for us now in those ages than we are to plant that yet unplanted for after-livers, had the seed of Abraham, our Savior Christ Jesus and his apostles, exposed themselves to no more dangers to plant the gospel we so much profess than we, even we ourselves had at this present been as savages, and as miserable as the most barbarous savage, yet uncivilized.

The Hebrews, Lacedemonians, the Goths, Grecians, Romans, and the rest—what was it they would not undertake to enlarge their territories, enrich their subjects, and resist their enemies? Those that were the founders of those great monarchies and their virtues were no silvered idle golden Pharisees, but industrious honest-hearted publicans [tribute collectors]. They regarded more provisions and necessaries for their people than jewels, ease and delight for themselves. Riches were their servants, not their masters. They ruled as fathers, not as tyrants, their people as children, not as slaves. There was no disaster could discourage them, and let none think they encountered not with all manner of encumbrances. And what hath ever been the work of the best great princes of the world but planting of countries and civilizing barbarous and inhumane nations to civility and humanity, whose eternal actions fills our histories with more honor than those that have wasted and consumed them by wars?

Lastly, the Portuguese and Spaniards that first began plantations in this unknown world of America till within this 140 years [1492-1631], whose everlasting actions before our eyes will testify our idleness and ingratitude to all posterity and neglect of our duty and religion we owe our God, our King, and country, and want of charity to those poor savages, whose countries we challenge, use, and possess, except we be but made to mar what our forefathers made, or but only tell what they did, or esteem ourselves too good to take the like pains where there is so much reason, liberty, and action offers itself, having as much power and means as others.

Why should Englishmen despair and not do so much as any? Was it virtue in those heroes to provide that doth maintain us, and baseness in us to do the like for others to come? Surely, no. Then seeing we are not born for ourselves but each to help other, and our abilities are much alike at the hour of our birth and minute of our death, seeing our good deeds or bad, by faith in Christ's merits, is all we have to carry our souls to heaven or hell; seeing honor is our lives' ambition and our ambition after death to have an honorable memory of our life; and seeing by no means we would be abated of the dignity and glory of our predecessors, let us imitate their virtues to be worthily their successors, or at least not hinder, if not further them that would and do their utmost and best endeavor.

CHAPTER NINE

Peace and War

1612 to 1622

AFTER DE LA WARR'S DEPARTURE *Jamestown was governed in quick succession by Percy, Gates, and a newcomer named Sir Thomas Dale. Whereas Smith had ruled with an iron fist, Dale's fist had spikes. His merciless policy included beatings for arriving late at work and for criticizing official orders; the punishment for stealing, adultery, or running off to the natives was execution. The colony that would give birth to American democracy was in those dark times a grim gulag of contract laborers working in irons for years for the smallest of offenses.*

The colony was now at war with the Powhatans, but it had formed an alliance with the Patawomeck. In a power play against Powhatan, mariner Samuel Argall abducted Pocahontas in March 1613, bribing an Indian named Iapazaws to lure her onto his ship. Argall then brought her to Jamestown. During the months in which the negotiations dragged on, whatever resentment she may have felt toward the English must have evaporated, for she fell in love with and married colonist John Rolfe in

April 1614. She was then about 19, he 29, and she had the same intoxicating effect on him that she had on many young men in the colony: "[It is] Pocahontas," he wrote, "to whom my heart and best thoughts are and have been a long time so entangled and enthralled in so intricate a labyrinth that I [could not] unwind myself thereout." The wedding had a calming effect on Indian-white relations.

Rolfe had arrived in Jamestown in 1610, and he started Virginia's first real cash crop with tobacco seeds acquired in the West Indies. The local tobacco was too acrid for smoking, but the Caribbean plants not only thrived in Virginia, they "smoked pleasant, sweet and strong" according to Rolfe. So with goodwill flowing, and the economy on a somewhat steady footing, Jamestown finally enjoyed a few years of relative tranquillity.

In the summer of 1616 Rolfe took his young wife (rechristened Rebecca) and their one-year-old son to England as part of a Virginia Company effort to gain favor with the crown. The publicity benefit of a charming Indian princess converted to an English-speaking Christian was too good to pass up. Smith had a final meeting with her there. On her return trip to Virginia in March 1617, she died, probably of pneumonia or tuberculosis. Rolfe returned to Virginia, where he remarried and became a member of the House of Burgesses. He died in 1622.

During the years of peace, several important events happened in Jamestown. In 1619, a ship arrived from England carrying 90 "young maidens" eager to wed colonists. This morale boost helped to correct a male-to-female ratio that was highly unsatisfying for the men, and it gave many of them a desire to stay longer than they might have otherwise. The joint-stock company that arranged this enterprise realized the only profits from Jamestown up to that point. That same year, the colony, with a population of 2,000, started a precedent-setting representative government—the first legislative meeting consisted of a governor, six councillors, and burgesses from ten plantations. Also in 1619, a Dutch ship arrived with the first black slaves in what would become the United States. These first blacks were probably indentured servants who were

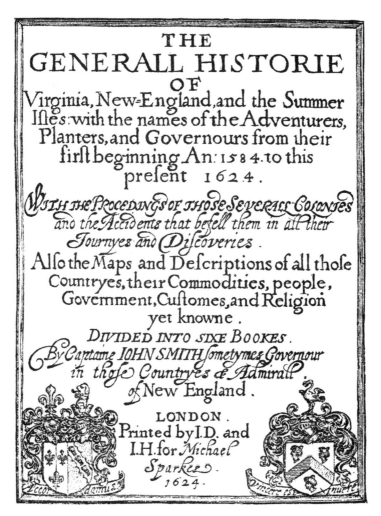

THE
GENERALL HISTORIE
OF
Virginia, New=England, and the Summer
Iſles: with the names of the Adventurers,
Planters, and Governours from their
firſt beginning An: 1584. to this
preſent 1624.

WITH THE PROCEDINGS OF THOSE SEVERALL COLONIES
and the Accidents that befell them in all their
Journyes and Diſcoveries.
Alſo the Maps and Deſcriptions of all thoſe
Countryes, their Commodities, people,
Government, Cuſtomes, and Religion
yet knowne.
DIVIDED INTO SIXE BOOKES.
By Captaine IOHN SMITH ſometymes Governour
in thoſe Countryes & Admirall
of New England.

LONDON.
Printed by I.D. and
I.H. for Michael
Sparke.
1624.

TITLE PAGE OF SMITH'S *GENERAL HISTORY* (1624),
WITH HIS TWO COATS OF ARMS

later freed, but within two decades imported black laborers were considered slaves for life.

The peace ended with shocking suddenness in 1622. As the English continued to come to Virginia in waves, the Indians were being pushed more and more off their lands. The many years of friendly relations had allowed the English to substitute complacence for vigilance. When Indians came into the fort on March 22, the colonists expected another day of normal trading. Some Indians even sat down to breakfast with their white neighbors. When the bloodbath began it was all-out brutal and spared no one—men, women, and children were tomahawked, shot, and beaten to death. By day's end 347 colonists lay dead, their fields burnt, their animals slaughtered. Jamestown reeled, and then struck back. A policy of extermination quickly replaced the kinder, gentler policy (that itself had replaced Smith's firm but fair attitude). The massacre served as a justification for taking over the country without regard for the natives.

Meanwhile, John Smith was busy with his pen. After he returned to England, he followed the news of Jamestown with interest and smugness. He had made a final voyage to the New World in 1614 and spent several months exploring the Massachusetts Bay area, naming the region New England; six years later the Puritans would land there at Plymouth.

Back in England Smith took up writing with the same zeal he had exhibited as an explorer and became a tireless exponent of colonization. Among his many publications, A Map of Virginia (1612) and The General History of Virginia, New England, and the Summer Isles (1624) were the most important. After the 1622 massacre, he offered to go over and bring the Indians to heel, claiming he needed only 100 soldiers and 30 sailors. The Virginia Company was not interested.

But when a crown commission on the reformation of Virginia requested his recommendations, he gladly obliged. When asked why the colony had not prospered since he left, he answered succinctly, "idleness." He also blamed the Virginia Company and advocated a poll tax on every British citizen to help finance the colony. It is unclear whether his suggestions were taken seriously, but in any event the Virginia Company's charter was revoked in 1624, and the company folded. The crown took over management of Virginia. What remained was Smith's reputation as the one who had, more than any other, added to the geographical and ethnological wealth of the Virginia area and kept the colony running when it was at its most critical stage.

VIRGINIA COLONY IN EARLY 1600S
(WOODCUT, 19TH CENTURY)

SINCE [CHRISTMAS 1611], THERE WAS a ship freighted with provision and forty men, and another since then with the like number and provision to stay twelve months in the country, with Captain Argall, which was sent not long after. After he had recreated and refreshed his company, he was sent to the River Patawomeck to trade for corn, the savages about us having small quarter but friends and foes as they found advantage and opportunity [*having only such relations with us as they found to their advantage, explains Barbour*].

But to conclude our peace, thus it happened. Captain Argall, having entered into a great acquaintance with Iapazaws—an old friend of Captain Smith's and so to all our nation ever since he [*Smith*] discovered the country—hard by him there was Pocahontas, whom Captain Smith's relations entitled the nonpareil of Virginia.

And though she had been many times a preserver of him and the whole colony, yet till this accident she was never seen at Jamestown since his departure, being at Patawomeck as it seems, thinking herself unknown, was easily by her friend Iapazaws persuaded to go abroad with him and his wife to see the ship. For Captain Argall had promised him a copper kettle to bring her but to him, promising no way to hurt her but keep her till they could conclude a peace with her father.

The savage for this copper kettle would have done anything, it seemed by the relation. For though she had seen and been in many ships, yet he caused his wife to feign how desirous she was to see one, and that he offered to beat her for her importunity, till she wept. But at last he told her, if Pocahontas would go with her he was content.

And thus they betrayed the poor innocent Pocahontas aboard, where they were all kindly feasted in the cabin. Iapazaws treading oft on the captain's foot to remember he had done his part, the captain when he saw his time persuaded Pocahontas to the gun room, feigning to have some conference with Iapazaws, which was only that she should not perceive he was any way guilty of her captivity. So sending for her again, he told her before her friends she must go with him, and compound peace betwixt her country and us before she ever should see Powhatan. Whereat the old Jew [betrayer] and his wife began to howl and cry as fast as Pocahontas that upon the captain's fair persuasions, by degrees pacifying herself. And Iapazaws and his wife, with the kettle and other toys, went merrily on shore, and she to Jamestown.

A messenger forthwith was sent to her father—that [since] his daughter Pocahontas he loved so dearly, he must ransom with our men, swords, pieces, tools, etc. he treacherously had stolen. This unwelcome news much troubled Powhatan, because he loved both his daughter and our commodities well. Yet it was three months after ere he returned us any answer.

POCAHONTAS AS CAPTIVE ABOARD SHIP ON THE
JAMES RIVER (19TH-CENTURY ENGRAVING)

Then by the persuasion of the Council, he returned seven of
our men, with each of them an unserviceable musket, and sent us
word that when we would deliver his daughter he would make us
satisfaction for all injuries done us and give us five hundred bushels of corn and forever be friends with us. That [*what*] he sent, we
received in part of payment, and returned him this answer: That his
daughter should be well used, but we could not believe the rest of
our arms were either lost or stolen from him, and therefore till he
sent them we would keep his daughter.

This answer, it seemed, much displeased him, for we heard no
more from him a long time after [*about a year*], when with Captain
Argall's ship and some other vessels belonging to the colony Sir
Thomas Dale, with a hundred and fifty men well appointed, went

up into his own river to his chief habitation with his daughter. With many scornful bravados they affronted us, proudly demanding why we came thither.

Our reply was: We had brought his daughter, and to receive the ransom for her that was promised, or to have it perforce. They nothing dismayed thereat, told us: We were welcome if we came to fight, for they were provided for us, but advised us if we loved our lives to retire, else they would use us as they had done Captain Ratcliffe. We told them we would presently have a better answer, but we were no sooner within shot of the shore than they let fly their arrows among us in the ship.

Being thus justly provoked, we presently manned our boats, went on shore, burned all their houses, and spoiled all they had we could find; and so the next day proceeded higher up the river, where they demanded why we burned their houses, and we why they shot at us. They replied, it was some straggling savage, with many other excuses; they intended no hurt but were our friends. We told them, we came not to hurt them but visit them as friends also.

Upon this we concluded a peace, and forthwith they dispatched messengers to Powhatan, whose answer, they told us, we must expect four and twenty hours ere the messengers could return. Then they told us our men were run away for fear we would hang them, yet Powhatan's men were run after them. As for our swords and pieces, they should be brought us the next day, which was only but to delay time; for the next day they came not.

Then we went higher, to a house of Powhatan's, called Matchot, where we saw about four hundred men well appointed. Here they dared us to come on shore, which we did. No show of fear they made at all, nor offered to resist our landing, but walking boldly up and down amongst us demanded to confer with our captain of his coming in that manner, and to have truce till they could but once more send to their king to know his pleasure, which if it were not agreeable to their expectation then they would fight with us and defend their own as they could—which was but only to defer the time to carry away their provision. Yet we promised them truce till the next day at noon, and then if they would fight with us they should know when we would begin by our drums and trumpets.

Upon this promise, two of Powhatan's sons came unto us to see their sister, at whose sight, seeing her well, though they heard to the contrary, they much rejoiced, promising they would persuade her father to redeem her and forever be friends with us. And upon this, the two brethren went aboard with us, and we sent Master John Rolfe and Master Sparkes to Powhatan to acquaint him with the business. Kindly they were entertained, but not admitted the presence of Powhatan. But they spoke with Opechancanough, his brother and successor. He promised to do the best he could to Powhatan, all might be well. So it being April and time to prepare our ground and set our corn, we returned to Jamestown, promising the forbearance of their performing their promise till the next harvest.

Long before this, Master John Rolfe, an honest gentleman and of good behavior, had been in love with Pocahontas, and she with him. Which thing at that instant I made known to Sir Thomas Dale by a letter from him, wherein he entreated his advice. And she acquainted her brother with it, which resolution Sir Thomas Dale well approved. The bruit [news] of this marriage came soon to the knowledge of Powhatan, a thing acceptable to him as appeared by his sudden consent. For within ten days he sent Opachisco, an old uncle of hers, and two of his sons to see the manner of the marriage, and to do in that behalf what they were requested for the confirmation thereof, as his deputy; which was accordingly done about the first of April. And ever since we have had friendly trade and commerce, as well with Powhatan himself as all his subjects.

Besides this, by the means of Powhatan we became in league with our next neighbors, the Chickahamanias, a lusty and a daring people, free of themselves. These people, so soon as they heard of our peace with Powhatan, sent two messengers with presents to Sir Thomas Dale, and offered them his service, excusing all former injuries. Hereafter they would ever be King James his subjects, and relinquish the name of Chickahamania, to be called Tassantessus, as they call us, and Sir Thomas Dale their governor, as the King's deputy. Only they desired to be governed by their own laws, which is eight of their elders as his substitutes. This offer he kindly accepted, and appointed the day he would come to visit them.

When the appointed day came, Sir Thomas Dale and Captain Argall with fifty men well appointed went to Chickahamania [Chickahominy], where we found the people expecting our coming. They used us kindly, and the next morning sat in counsel to conclude their peace upon these conditions:

First, they should forever be called Englishmen, and be true subjects to King James and his deputies.

Secondly, neither to kill nor detain any of our men, nor cattle, but bring them home.

Thirdly, to be always ready to furnish us with three hundred men, against the Spaniards or any.

Fourthly, they shall not enter our towns, but send word they are new Englishmen.

Fifthly, that every fighting man at the beginning of harvest shall bring to our store two bushels of corn for tribute, for which they shall receive so many hatchets.

Lastly, the eight chief men should see all this performed, or receive the punishment themselves. For their diligence they should have a red coat, a copper chain, and King James his picture, and be accounted his noblemen.

[*Smith being gone, his narrative becomes more scattershot. He includes a short piece by John Rolfe and colonist Ralph Hamor, an excerpt from a letter by Dale, and a summary of the lottery that the Virginia Company resorted to for raising money. We pick up the story as Smith is making one of his digressions about the administration of the colony; he then segues into a skirmish with the Chickahamanias (yet again over corn) and a letter he wrote to Queen Anne on Pocahontas's behalf. Pocahontas had sailed to England in 1616 with her husband and one-year-old son, Thomas. Following the letter Smith presents a curious account of his final meeting with Pocahontas, whom he had not seen since 1609, seven years earlier. The emotions remain unclear, though certainly she was upset that he had made no attempt to visit her until then. Possibly he was loathe to let her see her hero in his much reduced status as British commoner.*]

Now a little to commentary upon all these proceedings: Let me leave but this as a caveat by the way. If the alteration of government hath subverted great empires, how dangerous is it, then, in the infancy of a commonweal? The multiplicity of governors is a great damage to any state, but uncertain daily changes are burdensome, because their entertainments are chargeable, and many will make hay whilst the sun doth shine, however it shall fare with the generality.

This dear-bought land with so much blood and cost hath only made some few rich, and all the rest losers. But it was intended at the first the first undertakers [*colonists*] should be first preferred and rewarded, and the first adventurers satisfied; and they of all the rest are the most neglected. And those that never adventured a groat, never see the country, nor ever did any service for it, [*are*] employed in their places, adorned with their deserts, and enriched with their ruins. And when they are fed fat, then in cometh others so lean as they were, who through their omnipotence doth as much. Thus what one officer doth, another undoth, only aiming at their own ends, thinking all the world derides his dignity, cannot fill his coffers being in authority with anything.

Every man hath his mind free, but he can never be a true member to that estate that to enrich himself beggars all the country. Which bad course there are many yet in this noble plantation, whose true honor and worth as much scorns it as the others loves it. For the nobility and gentry, there is scarce any of them expects anything but the prosperity of the action. And there are some merchants and others, I am confidently persuaded, do take more care and pains, nay, and at their continual great charge, than they could be hired to for the love of money. So honestly regarding the general good of this great work, they would hold it worse than sacrilege to wrong it but a shilling, or extort upon the common soldier a penny. But to the purpose, and to follow the history:

Master George Yeardley, now invested deputy governor by Sir Thomas Dale [April 1616], applied himself for the most part in planting tobacco, as the most present commodity they could devise for a present gain, so that every man betook himself to the best place he could for the purpose. Now though Sir Thomas Dale had caused such an abundance of corn to be planted that every man had sufficient, yet the supplies [that] were sent us came so unfurnished as quickly eased us of our superfluity.

To relieve their necessities, he sent to the Chickahamanias for the tribute corn Sir Thomas Dale and Captain Argall had conditioned for with them. But such a bad answer they returned him that he drew together one hundred of his best shot, with whom he went to Chickahamania. The people in some places used him indifferently, but in most places with much scorn and contempt, telling him he was but Sir Thomas Dale's man, and they had paid his master according to condition. But to give any to him they had no such order, neither would they obey him as they had done his master.

After he had told them his authority, and that he had the same power to enforce them that Dale had, they dared him to come on shore to fight, presuming more of his not daring than their own valors. Yeardley, seeing their insolence, made no great difficulty to go on shore at Ozinies, and they as little to encounter him. But marching from thence toward Mamanahunt, they put themselves in the same order they see us, led by their Captain Kissanacomen, governor of Ozinies, and so marched close along by us, each as threatening other who should first begin.

But that night we quartered against Mamanahunt, and they passed the river. The next day we followed them. There are few places in Virginia had then more plain ground together, nor more plenty of corn, which although it was but newly gathered yet they had hid it in the woods where we could not find it. A good time we spent thus in arguing the cause, the savages without fear standing in troops amongst us seeming as if their countenances had been sufficient to daunt us. What other practices they had I know not. But to prevent the worst, our captain caused us all to make ready and upon the word to let fly among them, where he appointed others also he commanded to seize on them they could for prisoners. All which being done according to our direction, the captain gave the word, and we presently discharged, where twelve lay, some dead, the rest for life sprawling on the ground. Twelve more we took prisoners, two whereof were brothers—two of their eight elders—the one took by Sergeant Boothe, the other by Robert, a Pole.

Near one hundred bushels of corn we had for their ransoms, which was promised the soldiers for a reward, but it was not performed. Now Opechancanough had agreed with our captain for the subjecting of those people that neither he nor Powhatan could ever bring to their obedience, and that he should make no peace with them without his [Yeardley's] advice. In our return by Ozinies with our prisoners we met Opechancanough, who with much ado feigned with what pains he had procured their peace, the which to requite they called him the king of Ozinies and brought him from all parts many presents of beads, copper, and such trash as they had. Here, as at many other times, we were beholding to Captain Henry Spelman our interpreter, a gentleman had lived long time in this country and sometimes a prisoner among the savages, and done much good service, though but badly rewarded.

From hence we marched toward Jamestown. We had three boats loaded with corn and other luggage. The one of them—being more willing to be at Jamestown with the news than the other—was overset and eleven men cast away with the boat, corn, and all their provision. Notwithstanding, this put all the rest of the savages in that fear, especially in regard of the great league we had with Opechancanough, that we followed our labors quietly and in such security that divers savages of other nations daily frequented us with what provisions they could get, and would guide our men on hunting and oft hunt for us themselves. Captain Yeardley had a savage or two so well trained up to their pieces they were as expert as any of the English, and one he kept purposely to kill him fowl. There were divers others had savages in like manner for their men.

Thus we lived together as if we had been one people all the time Captain Yeardley stayed with us. But such grudges and discontents daily increased among ourselves that upon the arrival of Captain Argall, sent by the Council and company to be our governor, Captain Yeardley returned for England in the year 1617.

During this time, the Lady Rebecca, alias Pocahontas, daughter to Powhatan, by the diligent care of Master John Rolfe her husband and his friends was taught to speak such English as might well be understood, well instructed in Christianity, and was become very formal and civil after our English manner. She had also by him a child which she loved most dearly, and the treasurer and company took order both for the maintenance of her and it. Besides there were divers persons of great rank and quality had been very kind to her. And before she arrived at London, Captain Smith to deserve her former courtesies made her qualities known to the Queen's most excellent Majesty and her Court, and wrote a little book to this effect to the Queen, an abstract whereof followeth:

> To the most high and virtuous Princess, Queen Anne of Great Britain.
>
> Most admired Queen,
>
> The love I bear my God, my King, and country hath so oft emboldened me in the worst of extreme dangers that now honesty doth constrain me presume thus far beyond myself to present your Majesty this short discourse. If ingratitude be a deadly poison to all honest virtues, I must be guilty of that crime if I should omit any means to be thankful.
>
> So it is that some ten years ago being in Virginia, and taken prisoner by the power of Powhatan their chief king, I received from this great savage exceeding great courtesy, especially from his son Nantaquaus, the most manliest, comeliest, boldest spirit I ever saw in a savage, and his sister Pocahontas, the king's most dear and well-beloved daughter, being but a child of twelve or thirteen years of age, whose compassionate pitying heart of my desperate estate gave me much cause to respect her. I being the first Christian this proud king and his grim attendants ever saw, and thus enthralled in their barbarous power, I cannot say I felt the least occasion of want that was in the power of those my mortal foes to prevent, notwithstanding all their threats. After some six weeks [*actually three to four weeks*] fatting amongst those savage courtiers, at the minute of my execution she hazarded the beating out of her own brains to save mine, and not only that but so prevailed with her father that I was safely conducted to Jamestown, where I found about eight and thirty miserable poor and sick creatures to keep

possession of all those large territories of Virginia. Such was the weakness of this poor commonwealth, as had the savages not fed us we directly had starved.

And this relief, most gracious Queen, was commonly brought us by this Lady Pocahontas. Notwithstanding all these passages when inconstant fortune turned our peace to war, this tender virgin would still not spare to dare to visit us, and by her our jars have been oft appeased and our wants still supplied. Were it the policy of her father thus to employ her, or the ordinance of God thus to make her his instrument, or her extraordinary affection to our nation, I know not. But of this I am sure. When her father with the utmost of his policy and power sought to surprise me, having but eighteen with me, the dark night could not affright her from coming through the irksome woods, and with watered eyes gave me intelligence with her best advice to escape his fury; which had he known, he had surely slain her.

Jamestown with her wild train she as freely frequented as her father's habitation. [Wrote colonist William Strachey: "Pocahontas, a well-featured but wanton young girl . . . sometimes resorting to our fort (would) get the boys forth with her into the marketplace and make them wheel falling on their hands, turning their heels upwards, whom she would follow and wheel so herself naked as she was all the fort over."] And during the time of two or three years, she next under God was still the instrument to preserve this colony from death, famine, and utter confusion, which if in those times had once been dissolved Virginia might have lain as it was at our first arrival to this day.

Since then, this business having been turned and varied by many accidents from that I left it at, it is most certain, after a long and troublesome war after my departure betwixt her father and our colony (all which time she was not heard of), about two years after she herself was taken prisoner, being so detained near two years longer, the colony by that means was relieved, peace concluded, and at last rejecting her barbarous condition, was married to an English gentleman, with whom at this present she is in England; the first Christian ever of that nation, the first Virginian ever spake English, or had a child in marriage by an Englishman—a matter surely, if my meaning be truly considered and well understood, worthy a prince's understanding.

Thus most gracious lady, I have related to your Majesty what at your best leisure our approved histories will account you at large, and done in the time of your Majesty's life. And however this might be presented you from a more worthy pen, it cannot from a more honest heart. As yet I never begged anything of the state, or any[one], and it is my want of ability and her exceeding desert, your birth, means and authority, her birth, virtue, want and simplicity doth make me thus bold humbly to beseech your Majesty to take this knowledge of her, though it be from one so unworthy to be the reporter as myself. Her husband's estate not being able to make her fit to attend your Majesty, the most and least I can do is to tell you this, because none so oft hath tried it as myself, and the rather being of so great a spirit however her stature.

If she should not be well received—seeing this kingdom may rightly have a kingdom by her means—her present love to us and Christianity might turn to such scorn and fury as to divert all this good to the worst of evil, where finding so great a Queen should do her some honor more than she can imagine. For being so kind to your servants and subjects would so ravish her with content as endear her dearest blood to effect that your Majesty and all the king's honest subjects most earnestly desire. And so I humbly kiss your gracious hands. [In addition to doing Pocahontas a favor, Smith probably hoped that his diplomacy would help procure him a license for another expedition.]

Being about this time preparing to set sail for New England I could not stay to do her that service I desired and she well deserved.

But hearing she was at Brentford [*outside London*] with divers of my friends, I went to see her. After a modest salutation, without any word she turned about, obscured her face as not seeming well contented. And in that humor, her husband with divers others we all left her two or three hours, repenting myself to have written she could speak English. But not long after, she began to talk and remembered me well what courtesies she had done, saying, "You did promise Powhatan what was yours should be his, and he the like to you. You called him father being in his land a stranger, and by the same reason so must I do you." Which though I would have excused, I dared not allow of that title, because she was a king's daughter.

With a well-set countenance she said, "Were you not afraid to come into my father's country, and caused fear in him and all his people (but me)? And fear you here I should call you father? Tell you then I will, and you shall call me child, and so I will be forever and ever your countryman. They did tell us always you were dead, and I knew no other till I came to Plymouth. Yet Powhatan did command Uttamatomakkin to seek you and know the truth, because your countrymen will lie much."

This savage [*Uttamatomakkin*], one of Powhatan's council, being amongst them held an understanding fellow, the king purposely sent him, as they say, to number [*count*] the people here and inform him well what we were and our state. Arriving at Plymouth, according to his directions, he got a long stick, whereon by notches he did think to have kept the number of all the men he could see. But he was quickly weary of that task.

Coming to London, where by chance I met him, having renewed our acquaintance, where many were desirous to hear and see his behavior, he told me Powhatan did bid him to find me out, to show him our God, the King, Queen, and Prince, I so much had told them of. Concerning God, I told him the best I could. The King I heard he had seen, and the rest he should see when he would. He denied ever to have seen the King, till by circumstances he was satisfied he had. Then he replied very sadly, "You gave Powhatan a white dog, which Powhatan fed as himself, but your King gave me nothing, and I am better than your white dog." [*Uttamatomakkin came over with Pocahontas. Here he laments that the king treats him worse than a dog.*]

The small time I stayed in London, divers courtiers and others, my acquaintances, hath gone with me to see her that generally concluded they did think God had a great hand in her conversion. And they have seen many English ladies worse favored, proportioned, and behaviored, and, as since I have heard, it pleased both the King and Queen's Majesty honorably to esteem her, accompanied with that honorable lady the Lady De La Warr and that honorable lord her husband and divers other persons of good qualities, both publicly at the masques and otherwise, to her great satisfaction and content, which doubtless she would have deserved [*requited*] had she lived to arrive in Virginia.

The treasurer, Council, and Company, having well furnished Captain Samuel Argall, the Lady Pocahontas (alias Rebecca) with her husband and others in the good ship called the *George*, it pleased God at Gravesend [*on the Thames River, east of London*] to take this young lady to his mercy, where she made not more sorrow for her unexpected death than joy to the beholders, to hear and see her make so religious and godly an end. Her little child, Thomas Rolfe, therefore was left at Plymouth with Sir Lewis Stukeley that desired the keeping of it.

[*We skip forward five years to the massacre of March 22, 1622.*]

The prologue to this tragedy is supposed was occasioned by Nemattanow, otherwise called Jack of the feather, because he commonly was most strangely adorned with them; and for his courage and policy was accounted amongst the savages their chief captain and immortal from any hurt could be done him by the English.

This captain coming to one Morgan's house, knowing he had many commodities that he desired, persuaded Morgan to go with him to Pamunkey to truck. But the savage murdered him by the way, and after two or three days returned again to Morgan's house, where he found two youths his servants who asked for their Master. Jack replied directly he was dead. The boys suspecting as it was—by seeing him wear his cap—would have had him to Master Thorpe. But Jack so moved their patience, they shot him so he fell to the ground, [and] put him in a boat to have him before the governor, then seven or eight miles from them. But by the way, Jack finding the pangs of death upon him desired of the boys two things. The one was that they would not make it known he was slain with a bullet; the other, to bury him amongst the English. At the loss of this savage, Opechancanough much grieved and repined, with great threats of revenge. But the English returned him such terrible answers that he cunningly dissembled his intent with the greatest signs he could of love and peace. Yet within fourteen days after, he acted what followeth.

Sir Francis Wyatt at his arrival was advertised he found the country settled in such a firm peace as most men there thought sure and unviolable, not only in regard of their promises, but of a necessity. The poor weak savages being every way bettered by us, and [we were] safely sheltered and defended, whereby we might freely follow our business. And such was the conceit of this conceited peace as that there was seldom or never a sword and seldomer a piece, except for a deer or fowl, by which assurances the most plantations were placed stragglingly and scatteringly, as a choice vein of rich ground invited them—and farther from neighbors the better. Their houses [were] generally open to the savages, who were always friendly, fed at their tables, and lodged in their bedchambers, which made the

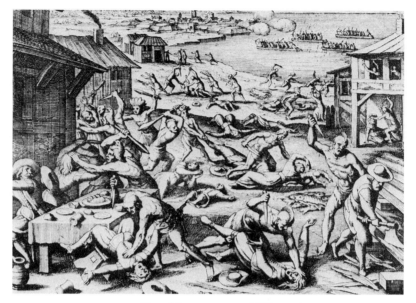

THE MASSACRE OF 1622
(WOODCUT, JOHANN DE BRY, 1561-1623)

way plain to effect their intents, and the conversion of the savages as they supposed.

Having occasion to send to Opechancanough about the middle of March, he used the messenger well and told him he held the peace so firm the sky should fall or [if] he dissolved it. Yet such was the treachery of those people, when they had contrived our destruction even but two days before the massacre they guided our men with much kindness through the woods. And one Browne that lived among them to learn the language, they sent home to his master. Yea, they borrowed our boats to transport themselves over the river to consult on the devilish murder that ensued and of our utter extirpation, which God of his mercy (by the means of one of themselves converted to Christianity) prevented.

And as well on the Friday morning that fatal day, being the two and twentieth of March, as also in the evening before as at other times, they came unarmed into our houses with deer, turkeys, fish, fruits, and other provisions to sell us. Yea, in some places sat down at breakfast with our people, whom immediately with their own tools they slew most barbarously, not sparing either age or sex, man, woman, or child, so sudden in their execution that few or none discerned the weapon or blow that brought them to destruction. In which manner also they slew many of our people at several works in the fields, well knowing in what places and quarters each of our men were, in regard of their familiarity with us for the effecting that great masterpiece of work their conversion.

And by this means fell that fatal morning under the bloody and barbarous hands of that perfidious and inhumane people, three hundred forty-seven men, women, and children, most by their own weapons. And not being content with their lives, they fell again upon the dead bodies, making as well as they could a fresh murder—defacing, dragging, and mangling their dead carcasses into many pieces, and carrying some parts away in derision, with base and brutish triumph.

Neither yet did these beasts spare those amongst the rest well known unto them from whom they had daily received many benefits, but spitefully also massacred them without any remorse or pity (being in this more fell than lions and dragons, as histories record, which have preserved their benefactors). Such is the force of good deeds, though done to cruel beasts, to take humanity upon them. But these miscreants put on a more unnatural brutishness than beasts, as by those instances may appear.

That worthy religious gentleman Master George Thorpe—deputy to the college lands, sometimes one of his Majesty's pensioners, and in command one of the principal in Virginia—did so truly affect their conversion that whosoever under him did them the least displeasure were punished severely. He thought nothing too dear for them. He never denied them anything, in so much that when they

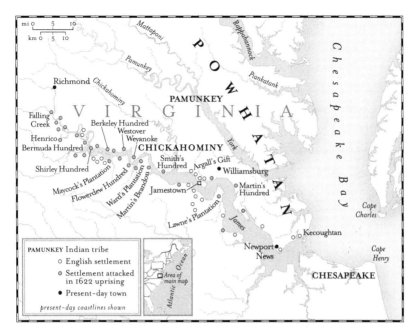

**ENGLISH SETTLEMENTS ALONG THE JAMES
ATTACKED IN THE 1622 MASSACRE**

complained that our mastiffs did fear them he to content them in all things caused some of them to be killed in their presence, to the great displeasure of the owners, and would have had all the rest gelded to make them the milder might he have had his will. The king dwelling but in a cottage, he built him a fair house after the English fashion, in which he took such pleasure, especially in the lock and key, which he so admired, as locking and unlocking his door a hundred times a day, he thought no device in the world comparable to it.

Thus insinuating himself into this king's favor for his religious purpose, he conferred oft with him about religion, as many other in this former discourse had done. And this pagan confessed to him as he did to them, our God was better than theirs, and seemed to be much pleased with that discourse and of his company, and to requite all those courtesies. Yet this viperous brood did, as the sequel showed, not only murder him, but with such spite and scorn abused his dead corpse as is unfitting to be heard with civil ears.

One thing I cannot omit—that when this good gentleman upon his fatal hour was warned by his man, who perceiving some treachery intended by those hellhounds, to look to himself, and withal ran away for fear he should be apprehended, and so saved his own life, yet his master out of his good meaning was so void of suspicion and full of confidence they had slain him ere he could or would believe they would hurt him.

Captain Nathaniel Powell [*veteran of Smith's second Chesapeake voyage*], one of the first planters, a valiant soldier, and not any in the country better known amongst them, yet such was the error of an over-conceited power and prosperity and their simplicities they not only slew him and his family, but butcher-like haggled their bodies and cut off his head to express their uttermost height of cruelty. Another of the old company of Captain Smith, called Nathaniel Causie, being cruelly wounded, and the savages about him, with an axe did cleave one of their heads, whereby the rest fled and he escaped. For they hurt not any that did either fight or stand upon their guard. In one place where there was but two men that had warning of it they defended the house against 60 or more that assaulted it.

Master Baldwin at Warraskoyack, his wife being so wounded she lay for dead, yet by his oft discharging of his piece saved her, his house, himself, and divers others. At the same time they came to one Master Harrison's house, near half a mile from Baldwin's, where was Master Thomas Hamor [*Ralph's older brother*] with six men and eighteen or nineteen women and children. Here the savages with many presents and fair persuasions feigned they came for Captain Ralph Hamor to go to their king, then hunting in the woods. Presently they sent to him, but he not coming as they expected, set fire of a tobacco house, and then came to tell them in the dwelling house of it to quench it. All the men ran toward it, but Master Hamor, not suspecting anything, whom the savages pursued [and] shot them full of arrows, then beat out their brains. Hamor having finished a letter he was a-writing, followed after to see what was the matter, but quickly they shot an arrow in his back, which caused him return and barricade up the doors. Whereupon the savages set fire on the house. Harrison's boy finding his master's piece loaded, discharged it at random, at which bare report the savages all fled. Baldwin still discharging his piece and Master Hamor with two and twenty persons thereby got to his house, leaving their own burning. In like manner, they had fired Lieutenant Basse his house, with all the rest there about, slain the people, and so left that plantation.

Captain Hamor all this while not knowing anything, coming to his brother that had sent for him to go hunt with the king, meeting the savages chasing some, yet escaped, retired to his new house then a-building, from whence he came. There only with spades, axes, and brickbats, he defended himself and his company till the savages departed. Not long after, the master from the ship had sent six musketeers, with which he recovered their merchant's storehouse, where he armed ten more, and so with thirty more unarmed workmen found his brother and the rest at Baldwin's. Now seeing all they had was burned and consumed, they repaired to Jamestown with their best expedition. Yet not far from Martin's Hundred [about seven miles east of Jamestown], where seventy-three were slain, was a little house and a small family that heard not of any of this till two days after.

All those, and many others whom they have as maliciously murdered, sought the good of those poor brutes, that thus despising God's mercies must needs now as miscreants be corrected by justice. To which leaving them, I will knit together the thread of this discourse.

At the time of the massacre, there were three or four ships in James River, and one in the next, and daily more to come in, as there did within fourteen days after, one of which they endeavored to have surprised. Yet were the hearts of the English ever stupid, and averted from believing anything might weaken their hopes to win them [*the Indians*] by kind usage to Christianity. But divers write from thence that Almighty God hath his great work in this tragedy, and will thereout draw honor and glory to his name and a more flourishing estate and safety to themselves, and with more speed to convert the savage children to himself since he so miraculously hath preserved the English, there being yet (God be praised) eleven parts of twelve remaining, whose careless neglect of their own safeties seems to have been the greatest cause of their destructions. Yet you see, God by a converted savage that disclosed the plot, saved the rest, and the pinnace then in Pamunkey's River, whereof (say they) though our sins made us unworthy of so glorious a conversion, yet his infinite wisdom can nevertheless bring it to pass, and in good time, by such means as we think most unlikely. For in the delivery of them that survive, no man's particular carefulness saved one person, but the mere goodness of God himself, freely and miraculously preserving whom he pleased.

The letters of Master George Sands, a worthy gentleman, and many others besides them returned, brought us this unwelcome news that hath been heard at large in public court, that the Indians and they lived as one nation, yet by a general combination in one day plotted to subvert the whole colony, and at one instant, though our several plantations were one hundred and forty miles up on [*up and down the*] river on both sides.

But for the better understanding of all things, you must remember these wild naked natives live not in great numbers together, but dispersed commonly in thirty, forty, fifty, or sixty in a company. Some places have two hundred, few places more, but many less; yet they had all warning given them one from another in all their habitations, though far asunder, to meet at the day and hour appointed for our destruction at all our several plantations—some directed to one place, some to another, all to be done at the time appointed, which they did accordingly. Some entering their houses under color of trading so took their advantage, others drawing us abroad under fair pretenses, and the rest suddenly falling upon those that were at their labors.

Six of the Council suffered under this treason, and the slaughter had been universal if God had not put it into the heart of an Indian, who lying in the house of one Pace was urged by another Indian his brother that lay with him the night before to kill Pace, as he should do Perry which was his friend, being so commanded from their king. Telling him also how the next day the execution should be finished, Perry's Indian presently arose and revealed it to Pace that used him as his son, and thus them that escaped was saved by this one converted infidel. And though three hundred forty-seven were slain, yet thousands of ours were by the means of this alone thus preserved, for which God's name be praised forever and ever.

Pace, upon this securing his house, before day rowed to Jamestown, and told the governor of it. Whereby they were prevented, and at such other plantations as possibly intelligence could be given. And where they saw us upon our guard, at the sight of a piece they ran away. But the rest were most slain, their houses burned, such arms and munition as they found they took away, and some cattle also they destroyed. Since, we find Opechancanough the last year had practiced with a king on the eastern shore to furnish him with a kind of poison, which only grows in his country, to poison us. But of this bloody act never grief and shame possessed any people more than themselves, to be thus butchered by so naked and cowardly a people, who dare not stand the presenting of a staff in manner of a piece, nor an uncharged piece in the hands of a woman. But I must tell those authors, though some might be thus cowardly, there were many of them had better spirits.

Thus have you heard the particulars of this massacre, which in those respects some say will be good for the plantation, because now we have just cause to destroy them by all means possible. But I think it had been much better it had never happened. For they have given us a hundred times as just occasions long ago to subject them. Moreover, [*he now seems to contradict himself*] where before we were troubled in clearing the ground of great timber, which was to them of small use, now we may take their own plain fields and habitations, which are the pleasantest places in the country. Besides, the deer, turkeys, and other beasts and fowls will exceedingly increase if we beat the savages out of the country. For at all times of the year they never spare male nor female, old nor young, eggs nor birds, fat nor lean, in season or out of season—with them, all is one. The like they did in our swine and goats, for they have used to kill eight in ten more than we, or else the wood would most plentifully abound with victual [*an interesting, if perhaps exaggerated, reversal on the idea that the Indians were better stewards of the land*]. Besides it is more easy to civilize them by conquest than fair means; for the one may be made at once, but their civilizing will require a long time and much industry.

[*Smith proposes to the Virginia Company that he lead a small armed contingent against the Indians. He summarizes the Company's reply.*]

If you please I may be transported with a hundred soldiers and thirty sailors by the next Michaelmas [*Sept. 29, 1623*], with victual, munition, and such necessary provision [*as*] by God's assistance we would endeavor to enforce the savages to leave their country, or bring them in that fear and subjection that every man should follow their business securely, whereas now half their times and labors are spent in watching and warding, only to defend, but altogether unable to suppress the savages, because every man now being for himself will be unwilling to be drawn from their particular labors to be made as packhorses for all the rest without any certainty of some better reward and preferment than I can understand any there can or will yet give them.

These I would employ only in ranging the countries and tormenting the savages, and that they should be as a running army till this were effected and then settle themselves in some such convenient place that should ever remain a garrison of that strength, ready upon any occasion against the savages or any other for the defense of the country, and to see all the English well armed and instruct them their use. But I would have a bark of one hundred tons, and means to build six or seven shallops, to transport them where there should be occasion.

Toward the charge: Because it is for the general good, and what by the massacre and other accidents Virginia is disparaged and many men and their purses much discouraged. However a great many do hasten to go thinking to be next heirs to all the former losses, I fear they will not find all things as they do imagine, therefore leaving those gilded conceits and dive into the true estate of the colony. I think if his Majesty were truly informed of their necessity and the benefit of this project, he would be pleased to give the custom of Virginia. And the planters also according to their abilities would add thereto such a contribution as would be fit to maintain this garrison till they be able to subsist, or cause some such other collections to be made as may put it with all expedition in practice. Otherwise, it is much to be doubted there will neither come custom [revenue] nor anything from thence to England within these few years.

Now if this should be thought an employment more fit for ancient soldiers there bred than such newcomers as may go with me, you may please to leave that to my discretion, to accept or refuse such voluntaries that will hazard their fortunes in the trials of these events, and discharge such of my company that had rather labor the ground than subdue their enemies. What relief I should have from your colony I would satisfy and spare them (when I could) the like courtesy. Notwithstanding these doubts, I hope to feed them as well as defend them, and yet discover you more land unknown than they all yet know, if you will grant me such privileges as of necessity must be used.

For against any enemy we must be ready to execute the best can be devised by your state there, but not that they shall either take away my men or anything else to employ as they please by virtue of their authority. And in that I have done somewhat for New England as well as Virginia, so I would desire liberty and authority to make the best use I can of my best experiences, within the limits of those two patents, and to bring them both in one map and the countries betwixt them, giving always that respect to the governors and government as an Englishman doth in Scotland, or a Scotchman in England, or as the regiments in the low countries do to the governors of the towns and cities where they are billeted, or in garrison where, though they live with them and are as their servants to defend them, yet not to be disposed on at their pleasure, but as the Prince and State doth command them. And for my own pains in particular I ask not anything but what I can produce from the proper labor of the savages.

I cannot say it [*their answer*] was generally from the Company, for being published in their court the most that heard it liked exceeding well of the motion, and some would have been very large adventurers in it, especially Sir John Brookes and Master David Wiffin. But there were such divisions amongst them, I could obtain no answer but this: The charge would be too great. Their stock was decayed, and they did think the planters should do that of themselves if I could find means to effect it. They did think I might have leave of the Company, provided they might have half the pillage. But I think there are not many will much strive for that employment, for except it be a little corn at some time of the year is to be had I would not give twenty pound for all the pillage is to be got amongst the savages in twenty years. But because they supposed I spoke only for my own ends, it were good [if] those understand[ing] providents [providers] for the Company's good they so much talk of were sent thither to make trial of their profound wisdoms and long experiences.

To conclude: The greatest honor that ever belonged to the greatest monarchs was the enlarging their dominions and erecting commonweals. Yet howsoever any of them have attributed to themselves "the conquerors of the world," there is more of the world never heard of them then ever any of them all had in subjection. For the Medes, Persians, and Assyrians never conquered all Asia, nor the Grecians but part of Europe and Asia. The Romans indeed had a great part of both, as well as Africa, but as for all the northern parts of Europe and Asia, the interior southern and western parts of Africa, all America and terra incognita, they were all ignorant. Nor is our knowledge yet but superficial.

By this you may perceive how much they err that think everyone which has been at Virginia understands or knows what Virginia is. Now this our young commonwealth in Virginia, as you have read once, consisted but of 38 persons, and in two years increased but to 200. Yet by this small means so highly was approved the plantation in Virginia, as how many lords with worthy knights and brave gentlemen pretended to see it—and some did. And now after the expense of fifteen years more, and such massive sums of men and money, grow they disanimated? If we truly consider [compare] our proceedings with the Spaniards and the rest, we have no reason to despair. For with so small charge, they never had either greater discoveries—with such certain trials of more several commodities—than in this short time hath been returned from Virginia, and by much less means.

As for all their particular actions since the return of Captain Smith, for that they have been printed from time to time and published to the world, I cease farther to trouble you with any repetition of things so well known more than are necessary to conclude the history, leaving this assurance to all posterity: How unprosperously things may succeed, by what changes or chances soever, the action is honorable and worthy to be approved; the defect whereof hath only been in the managing the business, which I hope now experience hath taught them to amend, or those examples may make others to beware. For the land is as good as this book doth report it.

Afterword

by John M. Thompson

AFTER THE MASSACRE OF 1622, Jamestown recovered and started
to grow again. Another massacre in 1644 left 500 dead, but by this
time the Indians were fighting a losing battle. Clearing the English
off the map may have been possible in 1607, but no longer. Virginia
was established. As for Jamestown itself, it slowly faded into the
pages of history. A rebellion in 1676 led by planter Nathaniel Bacon
against the royal governor, followed by another major fire in 1698,
did the town in. The government moved to Williamsburg in 1699,
and Jamestown was abandoned to the wind and weeds.

Jamestown today stands on a small island, tidal currents from
the James having washed away its peninsular neck. Ongoing exca-
vations continue to turn up revealing artifacts and skeletons, adding
to a collection of over 500,000 archaeological finds. The Jamestown
National Site displays a number of fascinating ruins, foundations,
wells, and items of daily use, dating back to the settlement's early

days. An adjacent history park, Jamestown Settlement, features a re-created palisaded fort, with a storehouse and armory; a Powhatan Indian village; and an exhibit gallery. And, most interesting of all, replicas of the three original ships are moored in the James River. Visitors may climb aboard these seaworthy vessels and listen to costumed interpreters discuss 17th-century seafaring life.

The Chickahominy River, just above Jamestown, remains a jewel, though development around Williamsburg is quickly increasing pollution pressures on it. The river winds down to the James between broad rice marshes, still providing some of the finest natural vistas in the Chesapeake system, as well as good fishing and great bird-watching.

The Pamunkey and the Mattaponi (the two forks of the York) also drain bottomland swamps, and they remain even less settled than the Chickahominy. Though they have few cypresses, they still have the abundant freshwater marshes that fed Opechancanough's people 400 years ago, and eagles and waterfowl still inhabit the area. Descendants of Powhatan's people continue to fish for shad in both rivers each spring, from the Pamunkey and Mattaponi Indian reservations, where both tribes operate shad hatcheries. The two reservations—the only ones in Virginia—claim a total of about 1,350 acres. About 34 families reside on the Pamunkey Reservation, with other tribal members scattered in Richmond, Newport News, and elsewhere, while some 60 of 450 Mattaponi tribe members live on the Mattaponi Reservation.

Today the James and the York still serve as working rivers, carrying naval ships, tugs with barges full of sand and gravel, and research vessels. Their utility, though, does not detract from their appeal—there is still enough of what John Smith saw in them to spark the imagination of the modern visitor.

As for Smith, in his last few years he chided colonists for having done little exploring since his time: "He is a great traveler," he scoffed, "that hath gone up and down the river of Jamestown, been at Pamunkey, Smith's Isles, or Accomac." Smith was now back in England, living beyond his means but enjoying a circle of admiring friends. As a celebrity, he was often entertained at the homes of aristocrats, but he never went in for the pastimes of the upper classes. A comrade in the Hungarian wars celebrated his workmanlike virtue: "I never knew a warrior yet, but thee / From wine, tobacco, debts, dice, oaths so free."

After surviving battles, storms, poisonings, wounds, and countless adventures, the old warrior died in bed in 1631. He had risen from humble origins, made something noble of himself through dint of will and personality, and gone on to symbolize the kind of swaggering self-reliant character that would become the American ideal. With his life, he said that the frontiers were full of riches—even if not of the metal kind—waiting for people willing to go out and boldly seize them. Unlike most people at the time, he could see the new land for what it was, a big continent brimming with possibilities, but only for those who took it on its own terms. The English way of doing things did not apply. Instead, a new egalitarianism, in which everyone did his share of the heavy lifting, was the only realistic path for success in America. Class counted for little in the New World.

Over the centuries, John Smith's reputation has risen and fallen with trends in historical writing, bottoming out after the Civil War along with Virginia history in general. His detractors consider him by turns bombastic, hyperbolic, a braggart, a liar, and an Indian killer. More recent writing holds him in high esteem as a brave pioneer, a natural-born leader, and one of America's most important founders. Somewhere in between lies the truth about a fascinating figure whose 51 years (1580-1631) spanned a time of exciting change around the world, as England stood on the threshold of imperial dominance.

It is impossible to know what the American colonies would have been like without Smith. Some scholars believe he was their leading founder, and that without him the English ventures in Virginia and New England would have failed. What is true is that he was the most successful early leader of Virginia and that in thoroughly exploring nearly 2,500 miles around the Chesapeake Bay he opened up a vast new territory for settlement. Exploration has always been a matter of having the bravery to go a little farther, to find out what lies beyond the next bend. Smith left his mark on Virginia by doing just that. We remember him partly because he was a colorful character and a robust teller of his own tales. But mostly we remember him because he had the gumption to go out and do something big, bold, and original.

APPENDIX

IN THE FOLLOWING DIGRESSION, *Smith elaborates on how to subject the Indians. He swaggers, yet with rough poetry and Biblical cadence. A list of necessities for the prospective colonist follows.*

AMONGST THE REST OF THE PLANTATIONS all this summer [1622] little was done, but securing themselves and planting tobacco, which passes there as current silver. And by the oft turning and winding it some grow rich but many poor. Notwithstanding, ten or twelve ships or more hath arrived there since the massacre, although it was Christmas ere any returned. And that return greatly revived all men's longing expectation here in England. For they brought news that, notwithstanding their extreme sickness, many were recovered and finding the savages did not much trouble them, except it were sometimes some disorderly stragglers they cut off.

To lull them the better in security, they [*the colonists*] sought no revenge till their corn was ripe. Then they drew together three hundred of the best soldiers they could that would leave their private business and adventure themselves amongst the savages to surprise their corn, under the conduct of Sir George Yeardley.

Being embarked in convenient shipping, and all things necessary for the enterprise, they went first to Nansemond, where the people set fire on their own houses, and spoiled what they could and then fled with what they could carry, so that the English did make no slaughter amongst them for revenge. Their cornfields being newly gathered, they surprised all they found, burned the houses remained unburned, and so departed. Quartering about Kecoughtan, after the watch was set, Samuel Collier, one of the most ancientest planters (and very well acquainted with their language and habitation, humors and conditions, and governor of a town), when the watch was set going the round, unfortunately by a sentinel that discharged his piece, was slain.

Thence they sailed to Pamunkey, the chief seat of Opechancanough, the contriver of the massacre. The savages seemed exceeding fearful, promising to bring them Sara [*identity unknown*], and the rest of the English yet living, with all the arms and what they had to restore, much desiring peace, and to give them any satisfaction they could. Many such devices they feigned to procrastinate the time ten or twelve days, till they had got away their corn from all the other places up the river, but that where the English kept their quarter.

At last, when they [*the English*] saw all those promises were but delusions, they seized on all the corn there was [*and*] set fire on their houses. In following the savages that fled before them, some few of those naked devils had that spirit they lay in ambush, and as our men marched discharged some shot out of English pieces and hurt some of them flying at their pleasures where they listed, burning their empty houses before them as they went to make themselves sport. So they escaped, and Sir George returned with corn, where for our pains we had three bushels apiece, but we were enjoined before we had it to pay ten shillings the bushel for freight and other charges. Thus by this means the savages are like, as they report, to endure no small misery this winter, and that some of our men are returned to their former plantations.

What other passages or impediments happened in their proceedings, that they were not fully revenged of the savages before they returned, I know not. Nor could ever hear more, but that they supposed they slew two, and how it was impossible for any men to do more than they did. Yet worthy Hernando Cortés had scarce three hundred Spaniards to conquer the great city of Mexico, where thousands of savages dwelled in strong houses. But because they were a civilized people, had wealth, and those mere barbarians as wild as beasts have nothing, I entreat your patience to tell you my opinion, which if it be God's pleasure I shall not live to put in practice, yet it may be hereafter useful for some, but, howsoever, I hope not hurtful to any. And this it is.

Had these three hundred men been at *my* disposing, I would have sent first one hundred to Captain Raleigh Crashaw to Patawomeck, with some small ordnance for the fort, the which but with daily exercising them would have struck that love and admiration into the Patawomecks and terror and amazement into his enemies, which are not far off. And most seated upon the other side the river, they would willingly have been friends, or have given any composition they could before they would be tormented with such a visible fear.

Now though they be generally perfidious, yet necessity constrains those to a kind of constancy because of their enemies. And neither myself that first found them, Captain Argall, Crashaw, nor Hamor never found themselves in fifteen years trials. Nor is it likely now they would have so hostaged their men, suffer the building of a fort, and their women and children amongst them, had they intended any villainy. But suppose they had, who would have desired a better advantage than such an advertisement, to have prepared the fort for such an assault—and surely it must be a poor fort they could hurt, much more take, if there were but five men in it dared discharge a piece.

Therefore a man not well knowing their conditions may be as well too jealous [careful] as too careless. Such another loopschans [entrenchment] would I have had at Onawmanient, and one hundred men more to have made such another at Atquack upon the river of Rappahannock, which is not past thirteen miles distant from Onawmanient, each of which twelve men would keep as well as twelve thousand and spare all the rest to be employed as there should be occasion. And all this with these numbers might easily have been done, if not by courtesy yet by compulsion, especially at that time of September when all their fruits were ripe, their beasts fat, and infinite numbers of wild fowl began to repair to every creek, that men if they would do anything could not want victual.

For the books and maps I have made, I will thank him that will show me so much for so little recompense, and bear with their errors till I have done better. For the materials in them I cannot deny, but am ready to affirm them both there and here, upon such grounds as I have propounded, which is to have but one hundred fifty men to subdue again the savages, fortify the country, discover that yet unknown, and both defend and feed their colony, which I most humbly refer to his Majesty's most judicial judgement and the most honorable lords of his Privy Council, you his trusty and well-beloved commissioners, and the honorable company of planters and well-willers to Virginia, New England, and Somer Islands [Bermuda].

Question 1 [*from a Crown commission for the reformation of Virginia*].
What conceive you is the cause the plantation hath prospered no
better since you left it in so good a forwardness?

Answer. Idleness and carelessness brought all I did in three
years in six months to nothing, and of five hundred I left, scarce
threescore remained. And had Sir Thomas Gates not got from
the Bermudas, I think they had been all dead before they could
be supplied.

*A particular of such necessaries as either private families, or single per-
sons, shall have cause to provide to go to Virginia, whereby greater numbers
may in part conceive the better how to provide for themselves.*

Apparel.
1 Monmouth cap [*flat round cap worn by sailors*]. 1s. 10d.
3 falling bands [*collars*]. 1s. 3d.
3 shirts. 7s. 6d.
1 waistcoat. 2s. 2d.
1 suit of canvas. 7s. 6d.
1 suit of frieze [*coarse woolen cloth*]. 10s.
1 suit of cloth. 15s.
3 pair of Irish stockings [*close-fitting breeches*]. 4s.
4 pair of shoes. 8s. 8d.
1 pair of garters. 10d.
1 dozen of points [*piece of twisted yarn used for buttons*]. 3d.
1 pair of canvas sheets. 8s.
7 ells of canvas to make a bed and bolster, to be filled in
        Virginia, serving for two men. 8s.
5 ells of coarse canvas to make a bed at sea for two men. 5s.
1 coarse rug at sea for two men. 6s.
4£. [*apparel total*]

Victual for a whole year for a man, and so after the rate
for more.
8 bushels of meal. 2£.
2 bushels of peas. 6s.
2 bushels of oatmeal. 9s.
1 gallon of aqua vitae. 2s. 6d.
1 gallon of oil. 3s. 6d.
2 gallons of vinegar. 2s.
3£. 3s. [*victual total*]

Arms for a man, but if half your men be armed it is well, so
    all have swords and pieces.
1 armor complete, light. 17s.
1 long piece five foot and a half, near musket bore. 1£. 2s.
1 sword. 5s.
1 belt. 1s.
1 bandolier. 1s. 6d.
20 pound of powder. 18s.
60 pound of shot or lead, pistol and goose shot. 5s.
3£. 9s. 6d. [*arms total*]

Household implements for a family and [*of*] six persons;
    and so for more or less after the rate.
1 iron pot. 7s.
1 kettle. 6s.
1 large frying pan. 2s. 6d.
1 gridiron. 1s. 6d.
2 skillets. 5s.
1 spit. 2s.
platters, dishes, spoons of wood 4s.
1£. 8s. [*implements total*]

Tools for a family of six persons, and so after the rate for
more.

5 broad hoes at 2s. a piece. 10s.

5 narrow hoes at 16d. a piece. 6s. 8d.

2 broadaxes at 3s. 8d. a piece. 7s. 4d.

5 felling axes at 18d. a piece. 7s. 6d.

2 steel handsaws at 16d. a piece. 2s. 8d.

2 two-hand saws at 5s. a piece. 10s.

1 whipsaw, set and filed, with box, file and wrest [*tool for
setting sawteeth*]. 10s.

2 hammers 12d. a piece. 2s.

3 shovels 18d. a piece. 4s. 6d.

2 spades at 18d. a piece. 3s.

2 augers at 6d. a piece. 1s.

6 chisels at 6d. a piece. 3s.

2 piercers [*awls*] stocked 4d. a piece. 8d.

3 gimlets at 2d. a piece. 6d.

2 hatchets at 21d. a piece. 3s. 6d.

2 froes to cleave pale [*stakes*]. 18d. 3s.

2 hand bills [*blade tools*]. 20d. a piece. 3s. 4d.

1 grindstone. 3s.

nails of all sorts to the value of 2£.

2 pickaxes. 3s.

6£. 2s. 8d. [*tools total*]

For sugar, spice, and fruit, and at sea for six men. 12s. 6d.

So the full charge after this rate for each person will amount
about the sum of 12£. 10s.

The passage of each man is 6£.

The freight of these provisions for a man will be about half
a ton, which is 1£. 10s.

So the whole charge will amount to about 20£.*

Now if the number be great, nets, hooks and lines, but cheese, bacon, kine [cows], and goats must be added. And this is the usual proportion the Virginia Company do bestow upon their tenants they send.

---

* A pound sterling was equal to 20 shillings; one shilling equals 12 pence. David A. Price's Love and Hate in Jamestown suggests an inflation factor of 134 between 1609 and 2001. Thus the whole charge of 20 pounds would today equal about 2,680 pounds. With an exchange rate of $1.70 to $1.90 to the pound, the amount would be $4,556 to $5,092.

INDEX

ACKNOWLEDGMENTS

SEVERAL PEOPLE AND INSTITUTIONS deserve credit for their help with this book. The University of North Carolina Press made the John Smith text available; in particular, rights and contracts manager Vicky Wells provided encouragement and much-needed technical assistance. Margo Browning put the text into workable shape and provided moral support. Working with the National Geographic Book Division map group, Justin Morrill contributed to the production of the fine maps and was a pleasure to work with. John Page Williams of the Chesapeake Bay Foundation helps keep the Chesapeake a splendid natural resource; his work with National Geographic was the genesis of this book. Nina Hoffman at National Geographic suggested the idea for the book, and Barbara Brownell Grogan supported it from its earliest stages and encouraged it along the way. Cameron Zotter designed the book; Susan Tyler Hitchcock proofread it—many thanks to both. And special thanks goes to project manager Garrett Brown, who deftly pulled all the pieces together from beginning to end.